NETWORKING
YOUR WAY TO
SUCCESS

10 Steps to Building Relationships & Expanding Your Business For Entrepreneurs & Working Professionals

BY DR. JAIRO BORJA

www.CelebrityMediaGroup.com

Networking Your Way to Success

www.BorjaConsultingGroup.com
Jairo@BorjaConsultingGroup.com

Published by: Celebrity Media Group
www.CelebrityMediaGroup.com

ISBN 13: 978-1-707640-69-0
Printed in the United States of America.

CONTENTS

INTRODUCTION

Who am I? I am just a kid from Corona, Queens, NY, living the dream. A Mets fan, (yes, a Mets Fan). I went to elementary school and middle school in Corona, Queens, NY. I also went to Thomas Edison High School in Jamaica, Queens, NY. I thought I was going to become an electrician after high school. However, halfway through the program, I knew that I did not want to do that for a living.

I was always fascinated with how money worked, how business worked. It is why I majored in business during college. I was meant for entrepreneurship but didn't know it yet. I bounced around between financial services, marketing, and eventually landed in higher education.

I worked as an instructor and taught several courses in business, including Small Business Management, Leadership, and Principles of Marketing. I also worked in higher education administration as a Career Counselor, Business Developer and Director of Business Development. I connected with companies to hire students for internships and career opportunities.

During my final year in higher education, completing my Doctor of Business Administration Degree in Marketing, I started my own consulting company, Borja Consulting Group. I did workshops on leveraging social media for business, leveraging LinkedIn for your everyday business, model business week, and how to network. I also helped small business start-ups with business coaching and business plans. As I assisted my clients, I realized that they had financial gaps. I partnered with a financial services company to assist my clients in addressing these financial gaps.

There you have it, how I went from Corona Queens to running two businesses.

Dedication

I dedicate this book first to God.

Without him, nothing is possible.

It also takes a village to make a doctor.

My family has supported me in my journey. To my wife Sofia, daughters Emilie and Emma, I love you.

My rock and biggest fan, my mother Carmen, I love you too. My brother Michael and my nephew, Sebastian, love you guys too. Couldn't forget my stepfather Lino and sisters Jennifer and Kathy, love you too.

Lastly, this book is dedicated to my father, Jairo Borja Sr. and grandmother Nidia Palacio who although they are not here with me today, will always be with me in spirit. I miss you both every day, love you too.

Before the Networking Event

Many things occur before the networking event. Whether you are an exhibitor or an attendee at a networking event, preparation is key. Your 30-second elevator speech should be on point. The 30-second elevator speech shouldn't be about yourself; it should be how you can help your audience. For example, usually, someone says, "Hello I am Joe, and I'm a financial planner!" It sounds ok, but as the person having a conversation with him, it isn't clear if he is a money guy or an insurance guy. A better conversation starter would be "Hello, I am Joe and I help individuals & businesses build wealth, protect assets, and manage cash flow!" What a difference, right? He never mentioned his title or any credentials. He only mentioned how he could assist with certain business pains. That is one example of how just tweaking the elevator speech can spark a conversation without creating any prejudice towards you at a networking event.

I know business cards are a relic of the past. However, I am still a fan of the tangible business card. I like writing specific notes on each card about where I can help or how they can help me. I usually collect a stack of cards at every event. Later at home, I sort the cards by priority of how these individuals can assist me in the short term and long term. I discuss this later in the book. For now, you should have a stack of business cards ready to go, ready to be exchanged at your next networking event.

Research before the networking event is a great idea. Sometimes when you register, you can see who else registers. This way, you have an idea of how to prepare and craft your elevator speech. You can also research the specific organization or chamber of commerce beforehand to see what type of audience will attend event. For example, if the event is all security professionals, you should be prepared to discuss guard service, cybersecurity, software integration, physical security, etc. This way, you have FORM (family-occupation-recreation-motivation) on lock, which we will discuss later in this book. At any networking event, it is about making connections. The highest chance for making a connection at any networking event is to know what you are talking about using FORM.

A whole separate book could be written about being an exhibitor, but for now let's keep it basic. You should, of course, have your point of sale items and props on point. Presentations and demos should be on point. The most important thing besides the product knowledge and the props for the table is what are you doing to attract attendees to stop by your table. Putting golf balls, basketballs, spinning wheels, etc. sounds cheesy, yes. However, relationships begin with FORM. The best way to establish any relationship is with FORM. That is how you make the connection, and then you can discuss your product or service. Many exhibitors that I have seen fail to make the connection with the attendee. I think it is important to have something to bring the attendee to the table, make the connection and then inform them about your product or service.

Being an attendee of any expo or event follows similar guidelines to being prepared at a networking event. Do you have your business cards ready? If possible, try to know who is attending in advance so you can tweak your 30-second elevator speech accordingly. At any event, you should be strategic. Have a realistic view of who you can do business with. One strategy I have used in the past is to get the program of the event or expo. Then I review which companies are, for example, in the northeast area. Only then will I approach the table. I can set up a sales call, and I can physically visit the facility so many advantages of dealing with a local organization, for me, at least. Now, if your product or service can be national or even international by all means, go for it. I am telling you what has worked for me in the past.

Lastly, dress the part. When in doubt, wear a suit and tie or business attire. I've seen it time and time again, people underdress or do not fit in with the rest of the crowd. Do your research; sometimes, you can contact the event planner for the dress code. Know that an event with attorneys or financial services representatives is most likely a suit and tie affair. As compared to a fashion event where you should dress trendy. Know your audience. My theme has been to create relationships by using FORM. To do that, you don't want to stick out like a sore thumb. The next chapter will discuss the FORM method further, and I want you to be a master of networking by the time you finish reading this book.

Understanding FORM

During the networking event, individuals can find it challenging to strike up a conversation. I've seen countless people who are more worried about the hors d'oeuvres than the goal of the event, which is to networking. I politely ask, "I'm sorry to interrupt, but I just wanted to introduce myself, I'm Dr. Jairo Borja." Simple right? Some people find it challenging to network. It is my job to assist my readers in becoming a networking master. Again, ask politely, "I'm sorry to interrupt, but I just wanted to introduce myself." Now what to say afterward, it's about FORM. Let's discuss in this chapter.

Family

People love talking about their families. Whether it is their kids, parents, siblings, or relatives, it is very easy to strike a conversation about each other's family members. For example, if you are at a security luncheon, everyone has an uncle or aunt or brother in some way, shape or form that works or lives somewhere. People love dogs, and they are part of many families these days. There is a commonality right there. You have something in common with someone you just met tonight. You can talk about how you have a Yorkie and how the other person has a Maltese. Who knows where the conversation goes? You can start talking about dog parks, dog hotels, common things dogs like to do, etc.

Lately, speaking of my daughters has struck as a great conversation starter. Fatherhood is one of the things of which I am the proudest. Why not leverage it to start conversations. I meet either recent parents or parents somewhat older than me at networking events. Our commonalities are that we both have kids. We have that connection. The conversation goes from daycare to sports to academics. I make sure to connect with everyone I meet, and then try to collaborate so that both parties can benefit mutually from conducting business with one another.

OCCUPATION

People love to talk shop. People love to converse about the different situations on the job. You can discuss common situations but of course, can't comment on some insider information. For example, years ago, before becoming a doctor, I was a banquet waiter. I would connect with friends who were waiters at other catering halls. We would discuss scenarios with different guests and how we handled it. Sometimes how we would have handled it differently, too. Whether it's hospitality or financial services or healthcare, some of the conversations are the same. Especially if you needed a degree or certification to do the job, you could connect with a person at a networking event regarding education; I'll discuss this later. You can speak about colleges and begin to strike up conversations based on colleges, curriculums, and best practices. Remember, it is one thing to discuss best practices as individuals. It is another to converse insider information regarding a company. I endorse best practices in security for example, but don't get into bashing what specific organizations do.

RECREATION

Individuals love discussing common hobbies or interests. For example, I love mixed martial arts and professional wrestling. If I figure out what the other person has the same hobbies and interests as myself, I can connect with that person for hours just discussing MMA and professional wrestling alone. Again, it is about making connections, building relationships, and hopefully, you can conduct business with each other down the line. Some of the easier hobbies and interests to bring up are sports, fitness, outdoors, and dining. Other hobbies and interests can include collecting classic cars, stamps, coins, vintage action figures, etc. Again, it is about finding common ground, bundling relationships and hopefully conducting business with each other at some point shortly. When I first started networking, I would be as conservative as possible — now, I understand that it more of a transactional relationship. Making that connection with someone is so important to me. Building relationships for over a decade is what made me successful in my old role. Currently building relationships by finding common hobbies and interests has helped in my business every day. What motivates an Individual? Motivation is explained in the next paragraph

MOTIVATION

What motivates individuals? You don't have to answer that now. However, finding common ground can be motivation. What motivates me, for example, is to strive for greatness so that I can live comfortably. I also am motivated to make money so that my daughters don't have to take out loans like myself to get through college. Others are motivated by money, getting out of debt, starting a business, starting a diet. Again, at a networking event, it is about meeting someone, making that connection, and finding a commonality that may include motivation. If both of you own several real estate properties, you can discuss that. Some of the common topics for real estate include purchasing property for investment, for rental income for a primary residence, for commercial space, etc. individuals get excited talking about their business, practice, or and real estate. However, these same individuals who see the defense of the financial plan can forget about disability income, wills, life insurance, etc. That's how you bring up those items if you are a financial adviser for example. You protect your assets; you can continue to build wealth and manage cash flow better. Find common ground with someone, find out what motivates them, what motivates you, and see if you have some of the same passion and some of the same things in common.

Now you understand what FORM is, and I gave you some examples with each letter of the acronym. The next step is to master the FORM method. However, I added two more letters to this acronym as important talking points: Education and Achievements. Although education can be discussed alongside your occupation, I want to separate it and examine it in more detail. Sometimes what you study is not relevant to what you are doing for work. Let's talk about in the next chapter.

Adding Education & Achievement

We understand the FORM Method now — Family, Occupation, Recreation, and Motivation. However, I added Education and Achievements which we will discuss in this next section.

Education

A great conversation starter is the recent completion of my doctoral degree. I am the first doctor in my immediate family. I use it at networking events like an ice breaker. Individuals at events then want to understand the Ph.D. vs. DBA difference, how was the program, and how is it relevant to your job or business. Sometimes you have common fraternities or sororities, honor societies, or the same colleges. Having a common ground in education, both Individuals at networking events can make that connection of being part of the same alumni network, have similar professors, and have similar values since both individuals graduated from the same college or university. Some occupations need a certification to start work; others don't require one. It is why I separated education from occupation. Alumni networks or even governing bodies who oversee the project manager professional, for example, once you pass these exams, the common ground at networking events is the ability to pass the examination and use what you learned in your everyday business.

ACHIEVEMENTS

Yes, you can say this is part of Motivation. However, in my example, I am motivated by a better life for my family. However, one of my achievements was obtaining my MBA and DBA. Another achievement can be that you are a black belt in jiu-jitsu — an amazing achievement. However, your motivation to get up out of bed in the morning may be money. That is why I separated Achievement from occupation or recreation as part of the FORM or now by reading this book FORMEA. Easy to remember, I hope. Examples of achievements can be 40 under 40, industry-specific awards, awards with your company, faith-based awards, nonprofit work, etc. Not only these are all great achievements, but also some great conversation starters. As a networker, you discuss achievements amongst each other, find common ground, build that relationship, and with the law of reciprocity, give referrals to each other.

You want to be known as a master connector. You want to help as many people as possible so that when you are the one that needs help, you have resources and individuals that are ready to help you. I know I have repeated it a few times, and it will be a theme in this book. Find common ground, build relationships, and then you will eventually make a sale based on the rapport you have established with the person you met at the networking event.

This chapter broke down the FORM acronym and added Education and Achievements as additional points of commonality. Hopefully, along the way, I have given you techniques on how to master the networking event. The next chapter is an interview with master networker Luis De La Hoz, enjoy.

Interview with Luis De La Hoz

The following is an interview with Luis De La Hoz. Here is a man who needs no introduction. If you are at an event, especially in the state of New Jersey, everyone knows Luis De La Hoz. Luis is the Chairman for the Statewide Hispanic Chamber of Commerce of New Jersey whose mission is to promote growth and development of New Jersey businesses and also assists members with expanded business opportunities through networking, mutual support, ties between private and public sector, advocacy for small business in the political process and lastly, promotion of trade for the New Jersey business community.

I had fun conducting this interview in New Brunswick, NJ. Enjoy:

Dr. Jairo Borja:

Thank you. Thank you. So for the listeners, for the readers, for that matter, tell them who you are and what boards or what's your capacity outside of your job.

Luis De La Hoz:

Okay. My name is Luis De La Hoz. I'm originally from Colombia. I moved to the United States in 2004.

Right now, I'm the vice president of community business development for BCB bank. I'm also the chairman of the board of directors for the Statewide Hispanic Chamber of Commerce. I belong to the board of directors of the Middlesex Regional Chamber of Commerce, the Puerto Rican Action Board, and the State Theater. Those are the boards that I belong to that I can remember. But my work is helping minority and small businesses to access to three things: access to capital, access to new markets, and access to a network.

Dr. Jairo Borja:

Okay. Good, good. Excellent. Thank you for that. So what does networking mean to you? Like whether it's personally, professionally, what does it mean to you?

Luis De La Hoz:

Ten years ago, I was not familiar with it, and I struggled because that was a word that many people mentioned to me that was key: networking, networking. But when I came from Colombia, for me, every time that a Hispanic individual mentioned networking to me was like a multi-level type of venture, right? Like Amway or networking marketing.

Dr. Jairo Borja:

Network marketing, right?

14

Luis De La Hoz:

And I didn't like it. And because I started working with not-for-profits since the beginning, I always mentioned to the people that I can not participate in those types of activities. Because that could be a conflict of interest now. I was invited to be part of BNI, Business Networking International, a couple of times. But I used to receive a very fancy letter from a financial advisor inviting me to a chapter, and I didn't pay attention. I was probably not able to read the entire letter.

Luis De La Hoz:

But I thought that that was $400,000 a month. And I say, I can not afford to be part of this group. This could be nice, but I didn't have the money to. Finally, I approached this big networking event with the local Chamber of Commerce. And I suffered. Like I was not prepared. I was not fluent. And I was having like pain on my neck and my back everywhere. Now, after the event finished. I was willing to go back home and tell my wife, if networking is a requirement, just pack. We are going back to Colombia. Even if we not allowed to because I don't know how I will be able to decode that.

Luis De La Hoz:

And a financial advisor approached me and said, "I'm Barry Jones, financial advisor Luis, you are really good." I said, what are you talking about?

Luis De La Hoz:

Like I have pain in places that I didn't know that I can have pain. But I say, no, no, no. You don't understand; this is not the best setup for you. Let's come with me to a meeting, and the meeting is tomorrow and just check it out. And I decided to go. I didn't know what to expect. I didn't research anything. As I say, I was in so much pain that I didn't. And I went. When I arrived, I realized that was a structure that allows me to learn and practice. And I was very surprised because they only allow you to three options every six months.

Luis De La Hoz:

Only three lates or three early. If you leave early, the meeting will be equal to one absence, you know? Basically you need to be there. Now one of the things that I realize is that that structure makes more sense than the Chamber of Commerce because, at the Chamber of Commerce, you don't measure a lot of things. But they measure attendance. How many referrals you give. How many referrals you receive. How many one to ones. And they mentioned to me that the networking process takes three steps. Visibility, credibility, and profitability. And they use this log-on called Givers Game. And you know many things get into to place. When I say, okay, this makes sense. I don't know how to do it, but this makes sense.

Luis De La Hoz:

I started attending the meeting. I used the meeting for more than just networking. I used the meeting as my board of directors. Let's say Louis De La Hoz Inc. I didn't have access to a board of directors. These meetings provide me access to a board of directors. The other thing is because English is my second language. Imagine how I was communicating ten years ago. Now, I realized that on my own business I was okay, but if I tried to go to a professional set up, I will sound like I came from the hood. And people will take purses or their wallets away from me when they hear me talk because [crosstalk 00:06:02]. But the reality was that I took that seriously. As people say in this country, I drank the Kool-Aid, and I become member. And I become a really good member, and that's surprised.

Dr. Jairo Borja:

Wow! Surprised. That's great.

Luis De La Hoz:

And what ended happening was this. That's, as I say, they offered me the opportunity to learn and practice. It's two aspects of the meeting. The meeting is every week, and every week I only have between 30 to 60 seconds to present my business. But every two or three months depends on how many members we have I do have the opportunity to make a presentation of like 10 minutes.

Dr. Jairo Borja:

10 minutes. Okay.

Luis De La Hoz:

Basically, I didn't know, but they prepare me for a TV interview. Why? Because I, in English, I don't have the resources that I have in Spanish. I try to get to the point. Right?

Dr. Jairo Borja:

Yeah, exactly.

Luis De La Hoz:

And the other thing is that I was able to improve my English because the meeting is one person per profession like Eric Morrell.

Dr. Jairo Borja:

He's an attorney.

Luis De La Hoz:

Right. It is four attorneys, one criminal, one corporation, one-

Dr. Jairo Borja:

One advisor.

Luis De La Hoz:

Yes. And the idea was that they were able to teach me how to say things that I did have the knowledge in Spanish, but I didn't know how to translate it into English. Now when that happened, I was able to communicate more efficiently and more professional. And that's what made the difference.

Dr. Jairo Borja:

Awesome. Good. Great stuff. Now you mentioned BNI, right? You're a big advocate for BNI, so why should an entrepreneur or business professional join a networking group, BNI, or [inaudible 00:08:14] or whatever the case may be?

Luis De La Hoz:

I will say because you need to learn and you need to practice. You know, I attend many networking functions, but I still go to the networking meeting. Why? Because you know, as many professional players, like football players, soccer players, whatever, they need to practice before they go. For me, that's the opportunity. Now I learn how to present my ideas in different ways that are more efficient. And I also can use analogies from one of your, that make a lot of sense for what I'm trying to do.

Luis De La Hoz:

And you know, it's very interesting because a lot of people have the knowledge, but when you have the ability to showcase your idea, and people understand what you say, what happened often to me is, I'm not the one who speaks the most. I'm not the one who ... but I can speak for five minutes, and I will have few people after I finish coming to me and say, I want to talk to you. You mentioned this you ... and I learned that the idea is not to try to push all my ideas out of my chest at once; it's just trying to provide people insights of what I want to talk about in order for them to approach me.

Dr. Jairo Borja:

Right, yeah. Good stuff. So, great stuff. I respect you as a great networker. So what makes you a great networker over the years, do you think?

Luis De La Hoz:

I think that I, as I say, I realize that it's not about me, it's about them. Right? I just passed one million dollars on thank you for close business that I've referred to their members.

Dr. Jairo Borja:

Uh-huh (affirmative), that's great.

Luis De La Hoz:

And I don't make the same amount of money. Right? But the opportunity to learn and practice through BNI gives me the chance. Last Sunday I was able to put together a meeting between the President of Columbia and the Governor of New Jersey. I realized that that was a big deal right? And last Monday, ... Not, yes, a week ago, they listed the most Influential people of color, and I was listed number four. And I feel like overwhelm and say, I don't deserve to be here. I have people under me, like Senator Menendez, Cory Booker, people that I admire and respect. Carlos Medina, like a lot of people that I respect. The mayor of Newark.

Luis De La Hoz:

But that was my feeling on Monday. But after we finished the meeting between the president and the governor, I feel like I do deserve to be there, I did a really good job. You know? And I dreamed this, and I created this on my mind two years ago, and this happened. And everything that I have been able to achieve happened because of three things. Networking, social media, and nonprofits. Those are the-

Dr. Jairo Borja:

Three reasons.

Luis De La Hoz:

-three reasons. Now, remember that I work mostly ... now I work with a financial institution, but I used to work with just nonprofits and none of them have a budget for advertising. I used to say that the only tools that I have to advertise the nonprofits are networking and saliva. Because that was the only two things that I can use a lot and nobody will complain about. But if I asked for a budget, they would say, no, no, no, no. We don't have budget for that.

Dr. Jairo Borja:

Exactly. So you're on a lot of boards. I'm on several boards. So why is it important for a professional entrepreneur to ... whether it's for [inaudible 00:12:19] or whether it's a statewide Hispanic, why is it important to volunteer professionally on a board like that, or even volunteer in general as part of your network or for networking purposes?

Luis De La Hoz:

Listen, nonprofits are really important in this country because ... you know the main difference between Latin America and the U.S. Is that you don't need to be from ... your last name doesn't need to be Kennedy to do well. You can be that house and do great things because people here, they don't know who you are. They really care about what you do, and what you know. Right? And how do you treat people?

Now when you are trying to advance something, nonprofits will give you the opportunity to be in front of people that care about the subject that is important for you. Right?

Dr. Jairo Borja:

Right.

Luis De La Hoz:

And usually, the people that you will meet at the board, are people that you are not able to meet on a regular basis. Right? Boards will give you the opportunity to get the information first hand and to disseminate the information to the people that really matter. Right?

Dr. Jairo Borja:

Yeah.

Luis De La Hoz:

And yes, I think that those are the main reasons, And the other thing is when I knocked the door at the statewide Hispanic Chamber of Commerce, and they say no to me three times. When Carlos came on board, and he came to the Hispanic Business Expo, he asked me, "Why are you helping them and you are not have us?" I say, "Because I knocked at your door and the people that were there before you didn't allow me to." And we say, "Okay can you help us?" I told him the only way that I will be able to help is if like I'm part of the board because I don't want to do the work and realize that in a board meeting they decide that the work that I was doing was not important for them. I told him I'm not getting any younger. I really want to do this for a long term commitment, but I just want to make sure that this is going where I want to go.

Luis De La Hoz:

You know, one thing that I learned here is that titles here are important. Not your last name, but your title. Like when I was listed as a loan officer, people didn't pay attention to me. When I was listed as a vice president, people start paying more attention to me. When I was vice-chair, a few people pay attention, and a few people don't. But when I was listed as chairman, more people pay attention. And basically with networking you will be able to escalate. Networking doesn't happen overnight. Right?

Dr. Jairo Borja:
Right.

Luis De La Hoz:

It's very interesting because if you review my Facebook profile versus my LinkedIn profile, I have probably four times more connections on LinkedIn versus Facebook. Why? Because Facebook will help you with visibility, but I don't get leads out of

Facebook. Right? But I do get leads, and I do get business out of LinkedIn.

Luis De La Hoz:

Is the main difference. Now the other thing is, I create the habit that every time that I go to a networking function, I will take a picture of the business card, I will add it to my database. You know I have like 11,000 contacts on my cell phone. And I remember when I resigned to the nonprofit the founder and the technical director was looking on my cell phone. They say, "Are you taking your cell phone with you?" I say, "Of course, it's mine." But everywhere I called to do number, and they didn't call to us. Yeah I'm sorry, but [crosstalk 00:16:12] introduce myself.

Dr. Jairo Borja:

You answered ... you kind of led into my next question is to how important is follow-up in a networking event or what techniques do you use? So you kind of started to elaborate on that a little bit. Anything else you do besides taking a picture and add it into your database?

Luis De La Hoz:

I think that it is important to pass on to you. And I don't know how I do it, but I have the ability to connect. If people express a need, or a pain to me, the way that my brain works is, I probably don't remember all the details, but I know, let's say that you asked me, "Hey, I have this problem." I would think like, okay, you will need this professional, or you will need this person. Or if you express to me that, I have this preference or I support, I didn't know. I love dogs, rescue dogs. Right? I will be able to connect with other people that have the same interest. And at the end of the day, that's what we do as human beings. You know, we don't want to talk about business every single day or the problems. We want to connect with people.

Luis De La Hoz:

And we have, as Ivan Pavlov says, we have one mouth and two ears, we better listen twice as much as we speak. Right?

Dr. Jairo Borja:

Right, exactly.

Luis De La Hoz:

It's hard for me if I'm doing that in the Spanish, but in English, I can do that because I tend to be introverted in English rather than extrovert.

Dr. Jairo Borja:

Makes sense. So you spoke about a little bit of social media. So what is the best way for an entrepreneur or business owner to leverage social media, whether it's before the event, during the event, or after the event? The best way to leverage social media, like the best way to use social media?

Luis De La Hoz:

For me, the way that I use social media is an extension of my face to face interaction. You know people ... it's very interesting because people call themselves influencers. And they call me asking me favors. Luis, but what are you talking about? Like you pretend yourself to me that you are this big deal. Right? Why do you care about me, that I'm not a big deal? Right? Now I'm promoting an event, and only 20 people register. But if you share it through your network, that would help me. Why do you think that that will happen? No. No, because you know many people is yes. Like right now, I'm not able to promote things when I'm not attending. Right? I can post it to the newsletter. Yes, but if you see a post and I say I'm supporting a hundred percent this event, you are expecting me to be there. And if you show up and I'm not there.

Luis De La Hoz:

Like today I have a problem. I was scheduled to be in Trenton, and I was not able to make it, and I get a few calls saying, "Hey, where are you? I came all the way here because I want to speak with you and you weren't." "I'm so sorry, I have this." Right? But in reality, as I say, chose an extension of the face to face. I had chosen a few people that I met them in social before I met them in person, but the majority of the people that I deal with, I will met them in person, and I will connect with them on social media.

Dr. Jairo Borja:

Okay, good, good. So how important, we're talking about social media. How important is social media to your overall brand?

Luis De La Hoz:

It's huge because I don't have an editor, I don't have a PR person. I'm everything right for myself, right? Now, as I say, because I do work mostly with nonprofits, they never had a budget to advertise. They never had a budget to hire a PR person-

Dr. Jairo Borja:

or a marketing person.

Luis De La Hoz:

-Yes. That's basically the reason because I tried to do everything on my own. Now social media allowed me to do a couple of things. One is to communicate and to promote. Two, one of the problems that many nonprofits have is that they don't have the opportunity to communicate the work that they do. And if I don't communicate what I do, it's like I didn't do anything.

Right? And this is basically one image that summarizes what you do? This was one of our keynote speakers at the Hispanic Business Expo, and he explained it this way. What relationships can do for your brand. Okay. Help solve problems, business relationships, personal connections. I refer to this as a face to face.

Dr. Jairo Borja:

Face to face. Right.

Luis De La Hoz:

All right? Get to know your customers by paying attention. That's the other thing is, let's say that you are telling me that you are writing a book.

Dr. Jairo Borja:

Write a book.

Luis De La Hoz:

Right. And let's say that you call me and say, "Hey Luis, I'm ready to launch my book. And I happen to know someone that can interview you about your book. If I made that introduction, basically I was paying attention to-

Dr. Jairo Borja:

To me.

Luis De La Hoz:

Yes. I won't get anything in relation. It's not a transaction thing, but I will help you and helping you, you know, is the gold. Now Givers Gain philosophy is, as I say, it's not a transaction. I don't expect that every time that I help you, you will help me back. No. Sometimes if I can help you three times and one day, I will call and say, "Jairo, can we do this together?" And you say yes or no, but you will be in a better attitude with me if I already help you than if I-

Dr. Jairo Borja:

Of course.

Luis De La Hoz:

And those other thing is sometimes I get called, "Hey Luis can you call this person? I am trying to reach out to him, and he didn't answer it." I say, "Okay, but just telling me about it. Every time that you call him, what did you ...?" "No, no, I call him about sponsorship." "Yes. Like Jairo is not answering because every time that you called that answer will cost him 500 or a thousand. Like he's looking at his phone and say, "You know what, I better pass this"-

Dr. Jairo Borja:

Call, right.

Luis De La Hoz:

Now you will be regarded for guidance and recommendations. Let's give guidance and provide information. Now, this is the thing it's, and I did everything before I jump into the familiar.

Dr. Jairo Borja:

Yeah. Right.

Luis De La Hoz:

Right?

Dr. Jairo Borja:

Yeah, yeah.

Luis De La Hoz:

Now. You don't expect me to say that I suck about the services that I provide. Right? But if someone that you trust is telling you that I did a good job, you will have a better perception of the services that I provide, that I am telling you, "Hey, I'm really good about this." Right?

Dr. Jairo Borja:

Absolutely. Absolutely.

Luis De La Hoz:

Okay. Contribute to conversations. Like I do have people that I know, when I'm doing a Meet the

Lender's event, or accessing capital event, I have a group of people. I have another group of people that are interested on networking. I have another group of people that are looking for procurements or access to new markets. I know who is looking for access to the general market, who are looking for the Hispanic market, and how we can interact those needs in order for them to help each other. Those are the type of things.

Dr. Jairo Borja:

Okay.

Luis De La Hoz:

Now we are going to sales. But many people, they work-

Dr. Jairo Borja:

Straight backwards

Luis De La Hoz:

- opposite, yes. Without a sale, they don't want to have a conversation. And watch for the right moment to connect with your consumers. Listen to your consumer's needs in social channels. One of the things is we have members that they come to us and say, "I want to sell [inaudible 00:24:53]." "Do you have a liquor license?" "No, I don't." You know, "We can not help you to do that." But sometimes someone will say,

"Hey, I'm opening a liquor license." Now we can make a connection. I know at a restaurant in New Brunswick that is looking for a liquor license. You having trouble with a liquor license. Can we make this happen?" Those are the type of things.

Luis De La Hoz:

Usually, people would express a pain or needs. And if you pay attention and make those connections. And I think that the reason because people keep calling me is because I'm able to connect those dots.-

Dr. Jairo Borja:

Right, connect those dots.

Luis De La Hoz:

Yes. And they are not expecting that every time that I make that connection, they need to pay me. You know, they do that I do that generally because I really want to help. That's why sometimes people call me and say, "Do you know a plumber? And I say, "Do you use Google?" They say, "No, no, no. I prefer to call you because I know that you will refer me to the best." "But you live in [inaudible 00:25:51]. I never been there. Like it's difficult for me. No, no, but I know. Yeah. But in some cases I'm capable or willing to do it. If it's something that doesn't require the physical presence of the person, you know, they signed a piece of advice or whatever.

Luis De La Hoz:

Or the person, "Listen I need a lawyer, and I need a lawyer regarding immigration, and I'm willing to travel anywhere." It's okay. Those are the options.

Dr. Jairo Borja:

Okay, good. Last question. Any final thoughts for whether you're a business owner, or whether you're a business professional about our conversation of what should they take away from reading this chapter of our transcript here?

Luis De La Hoz:

For me, that working is about relationships. Focus on build relationships. Don't necessarily focus on the transactions. You never know where people will be. You know, the person that you met that was working as a bouncer could be a loan officer tomorrow. And that will be the person that will help you. Right? You don't know who people know? And I'm surprised, like members that I've been helping for many years, they make introductions for me that I didn't believe. But that was the only common person that I have with a big opportunity and a person that I know. And as I say, treat people with respect and try to help as many people as you can. You never will regret that.

Luis De La Hoz:

And if you focus on developing the relationships, you know? Relationships are like when you start dating. Not everything is good. Sometimes you messed up, but people … If people like you they will understand. But if they know that every time that you have an appointment you arrive late, or that you, constant last minute, or whatever, if people get the sense that that is your personality, that you must never change. And if you wonder why they don't call me or why then … you know, this is very funny for me right, it happened very often because they say "Your job is really easy. You get dressed, and you take a lot of pictures." Yes.

Luis De La Hoz:

Do you think that, that picture happened because we just wake up early this morning? Listen, do you know how many emails? Do you know how many phone calls? Do you know how many face to face meetings we have before we can do an event? Like this is what you see, what we can not brag about, hey, the struggles that we have when we put something together.

Luis De La Hoz:

My message is perseverance, discipline. I think that those are the key things that make a difference for me. And as I say, a lot of people see things that are happening now, but they never saw this struggle-

Dr. Jairo Borja:

The struggle behind it, right.

Luis De La Hoz:

Ten years ago when trying to bring 20 people together for an event was like a struggle.

Dr. Jairo Borja:

The struggle.

Luis De La Hoz:

That was so difficult. Now it's different. Now I have the people is like nothing, but it's because, during those ten years, we were able to build the relationship.

Dr. Jairo Borja:

Right. Good. I thank you Luis. I appreciate your time today. It's been a pleasure, and thank you. You bring great value to the book, and hopefully people learn something in the book. Thank you so much.

Luis De La Hoz:

Yes, and if you want this I can email the video.

Dr. Jairo Borja:

Yes, absolutely. Thank you so much.

Luis De La Hoz:

He's a really good guy.

Dr. Jairo Borja:

Thank you. Thank you so much.

I had fun conducting this interview with Luis De La Hoz. I learned that his network, his brand was not built overnight. He has worked for over ten years of networking and assisting the Hispanic community. Despite knowing almost everyone in the state of New Jersey, Luis still manages time to participate in the weekly BNI networking group. Also, focus on building relationships. Don't make it transactional. Get to know your business partners and focus on making the connection with each of the individuals in your network.

CHECKLIST DURING THE EVENT & QUIZ

Have you dressed appropriately for the event?

Do you have the exact address of the event?

1) Name three things you should do before the networking event?

2) What does FORM stand for?

3) Why did Dr. Borja add Education and Achievements separate to FORM acronym?

4) What is the law of reciprocity?

5) Name one tactic for networking mentioned during an explanation for FORM?

6) Why is making a connection important to building rapport with a person at a networking event?

During the Networking Event. Tips on Navigating Event

By this point, you understand the importance of FORMEA and how you can strike up a conversation. Also, make that connection with someone worthwhile for both parties to exchange information. You can exchange information via business cards or even via LinkedIn. When I first started networking, I was too aggressive and would want to give out my business card right after I started a conversation. Looking back, that was not the best strategy. Today, I try not to mention job titles or credentials, at least in the opening line. I am not a hypocrite. Education and achievements are great conversation topics. I mention what I do now to address pain points. I help businesses and individuals build wealth, manage cash flow, and protect assets. However, my clients have concerns financially, and my job is to address these concerns. How does that sound? I did not mention being a financial planner or having a doctorate. I learned the hard way; it is not about me. It's what you can do for individuals and businesses. Your elevator speech should have no job titles, no credentials, no designations. Your elevator speech should have what you do and what you do to address a pain point.

Do we understand elevator speech now? I think I did a great job explaining it, but why do I continue to mention it? Just because we understand what FORMEA is, doesn't mean that we are networking masters, just yet. For a networking event, the elevator speech must be understood. The 30-second elevator speech is one of your most important tools at a networking event.

Ok, now let's fast forward to being at a networking event or networking setting. What are some great tips?

Tip#1 Don't be afraid to interrupt group conversations. The purpose of the event is to network, to hopefully exchange business down the line. People are afraid to interrupt conversations in circles. Don't be afraid. Just say, "excuse me, I am sorry to interrupt, my name is Jane Doe, how you are?" That's it. Now you are part of the circle and can use the FORM strategy to strike a conversation.

Tip#2 Don't be with someone too long. Build rapport, yes. However, don't stay talking to someone too long. Talk to someone for about 5 minutes and then work the room. What happens is you miss out on opportunities to network with other professionals. I know the conversation is great, but you are there to network with several professionals.

40

Tip#3 Know your audience. You don't know too much about the audience at hand, I have googled something quickly, and I've been able to connect using FORM method with the audience at networking events. You don't have to know everything. You have to know enough to have a conversation. You don't have to be an expert in the field. At any networking event, it is important to know your audience. It will help to build a rapport with the people you meet at the networking event.

Tip#4 Don't hold up the wall, mix and mingle. Firm handshake and eye contact. I have seen it at parties, I have seen it at events. Individuals by the wall or by the catering and not mingling with other guests at networking events. It hurts me like someone scratching an old school chalkboard. Don't worry too much about catering. GET OUT and NETWORK. A firm handshake is so important. It projects confidence, and I can't stand the dead fish handshake or sweaty palm handshake. Take two seconds to wipe your hands and have a firm handshake, look someone in the eye and say, "Nice to meet you." Simple as that. Nonverbal communication is just as important as understanding FORM. Being on your phone against the wall seems like you are disengaged. Be engaging, put the phone away, and GET OUT and NETWORK. Remember, firm handshake, look someone in the eyes and say, "Hi, I'm Jane doe nice to meet you; what is your name?" You can repeat their name three times to try and memorize it. I've been bad with names, but I am getting better with that tactic of repeating people's names at networking events to assist me memorizing names.

Tip#5 You can network with a friend, but don't be too cliquey. Another pet peeve of mine is when people go to networking events and stay in their cliques. If you are not there to network, get out of there. You can go with a friend. However, separate at times. You don't want to intimidate someone who may not have read this book and does not know how to approach different groups. I jest, of course, and, understandably, you want to be able to have fun at a networking event with your friend, but it's not a hangout. It is a networking event, and hopefully you can do future businesses with those people in the room.

Tip#6 For speakers and panelists, take the program. For speakers and panelists, I take the program, and I connect with them on LinkedIn. While connecting with them on LinkedIn, I mention a part of the presentation I liked. Yes, I was paying attention during the presentation. Connecting with presenters will also allow me to connect with them for future business or programming.

Tip#7 At an expo, you don't have to talk to every single exhibitor. In my previous role, it was more advantageous to speak to companies in the New York/ New Jersey area. I looked at any program, and I made sure companies I was approaching were local. If you can do business with everyone, by all means, talk to every table. However, to be strategic, you should approach tables that you know you can visit in person shortly. This tip is just my approach.

Tip#8 Have enough business cards, and if you run out, connect with them on LinkedIn. You should have at least 25-30 business cards for any event. If you are at an expo, you should have 75-100 business cards. If you run out, it's ok. Just make sure you can connect with everyone via LinkedIn. This way you can follow up with them in the next few days.

So there you have it. The elevator speech and we also went over the eight tips during the networking event. The next chapter talks about organizing the business cards you collected and leveraging a CRM system. You are becoming networking masters. You have learned FORMEA, elevator speech and tips during the networking event.

Organizing Business Cards and Leveraging CRM

If you are reading this chapter, you have probably read about preparing for the networking event and understanding the FORMEA method. I have also taught you techniques of how to approach and strike up conversations at networking events. Now that you have business cards, what do you do with them?

I create two piles, short term and long term. The short-term pile becomes a list of contacts that I can contact in the short term. I can do business with this pile of contacts in the short term. The other pile is long term, and although I won't do business with them in the short term, I may do something with them in the long term. A small caterer of empanadas just starting their business on the side, I may not do business with them now. However, I have several events throughout the year, and down the line, I may use an empanada caterer.

What else do I do with my business cards post an event? I try to connect with them on LinkedIn. Now that you can use LinkedIn on your mobile device, if I ever need something from any of them, I can send them a direct message on LinkedIn. Also, I can promote my products and services on LinkedIn for all of my connections to see. My new connections can also see my work on LinkedIn, and they can do future business with me. I can post pictures, videos, share articles, and my new connections can view my LinkedIn summary. My summary represents me when I am not online. My LinkedIn summary summarizes what I do to new connections, and they can understand how to work with me. That is why I connect with all of the new connections that I met at a networking event on LinkedIn.

Just some other tips on LinkedIn. Please have a professional picture. Your profile represents you 24 hours a day, seven days per week. If you don't have a professional picture, then at least have someone take a photo of you against the wall from the shoulder up. You do not want a picture with your friends from Friday night as your default picture. I would also add any certifications or designations to your profile. Your profile represents you all the time, and you want professionals to know what you are an expert in. Also, any volunteer work, whether it's professionally for a fraternity, sorority, honor society, or board, should go on your profile. Volunteering professionally shows that you take time out of your schedule to volunteer and give back to fulfill mission of the organization. Besides, mention any volunteering you do for nonprofits as well. Companies and individuals respect those who take time off their schedule to volunteer and give back to fulfill the mission of the organization. I would add under volunteer experience. Goes back to FORMEA and making connections with these companies even if it is online.

Emails still work. What I have done in the past is to send a personal email to all of the candidates I met. Similar to a job interview, I say, "It was a pleasure meeting you at the networking event. I was particularly interested in (and you can highlight something you were talking about at the networking event)." This tactic will make you stick out at the networking event. Also, you can meet all of these new contacts for coffee/ tea or lunch and see how can both parties collaborate on future projects. My advice would be to try to see these new contacts in the next 3-4 weeks. I would try to set time on the calendar to try and meet them in your office. If that is not possible, then in their office. If that is not possible, then you may meet for coffee & tea.

Another tactic I do is I take a picture of all of my business cards and upload them to an application such as Camcard. The great thing about an application such as Camcard is I can take a picture of a business card, and I can upload it to Camcard. Camcard automatically would save it under my contacts on mobile phone. I can then export these contacts on to a customer relationship management software (CRM), and I can then add them as a contact there. I can add them to email campaigns for initiatives I am trying to push.

I use Hubspot for my CRM. I upload all of my contacts and any interaction with any clients or prospects, and I would add comments for any interaction with prospects and clients. Also, I can send emails from my CRM as well. I am making it easier to follow up. Speaking of follow up, I can also set up alerts to follow up with client or prospects down the line. This way I have certain touchpoints throughout the year with clients and prospects. What I do is anyone I meet at networking events; I upload on to HubSpot. I can then add them to email campaigns shortly. Speaking of email campaigns, I use mail chimp for email marketing. I can time emails to be sent at certain times. Also, I can set up ongoing campaigns to promote a newsletter of the latest products and services. You can set up campaigns to go out to your tier 1 or tier 2 clients. You can send a separate campaign to prospects as well. What is great about this is the mass reach. You can work on customized proposals, and you can have this email campaign work for you while it is sent out at some point the next day.

In conclusion, we have leveraged FORMEA and now am looking at the post-event breakdown.it is important to separate piles of short term contacts vs.

long term contacts. Also, connect with everyone on LinkedIn. Maintain your professional profile. Make sure you contact your new connections and set up appointments to meet with them in the next few weeks. Use an application such as Camcard to upload contacts automatically and eventually upload to your CRM. Using the CRM you can leverage these contacts for your CRM and create different email campaigns for your clients and prospects.

INTERVIEW WITH VICTORIA RODRIGUEZ

Victoria Jenn Rodriguez is the CEO of VJR enterprises and founder of The Female Collaborative. VJR Enterprises is a talent management consulting company dedicated to elevating, enriching, and empowering people to become the best version of themselves. The Female Collaborative is the go to network for women who strive to be happy regardless of their flaws. The organization focuses on growth, mind elevating and learning from others.

Here is the interview with Victoria Rodriguez. I asked all of my participants for this book almost the same questions. However, the open-ended questions allowed for probing for certain questions. I loved the answers I got from all the participants. Enjoy the interview:

Dr. Jairo Borja:

I know. I know. A lot of stress. I know. I know. I know. I'll get right to it. I don't want to take up too much of your time. For the sake of the book, just tell everyone ... well, first, let me take a step back. This is Dr. Jairo Borja, and this is the book, 'Networking Your Way to Success,' 10 tips for entrepreneurs, and also fitness professionals. How to improve their networking. Tell everyone who you are for the purpose of the book, and what boards ... or what do you do as far as what you serve on?

V. Rodriguez:

Sure. I am a motivational speaker and executive coach with VJR Enterprises. It's definitely a blessing. I truly feel my purpose is to help people become the best version of themselves, and I do that a number of ways. I have a consulting practice where I work with an institution to build out strategic campaigns on how they can attract, develop, and engage talent both in and outside of the organization. I also have a nonprofit that focuses on revolutionizing how women work and do business together. And so that really dedicated professionals in color and very vulnerable standpoint. And the reasoning for that is a really empowered people comfortable in their own skin. And so until out of board service, I served on one board in addition to the nonprofit board that I run global learning for girls particle in the South Bronx. It is an all-girls school focused on self-esteem focused on rigorous curriculum and getting the next generation of global female.

Dr. Jairo Borja:

That's awesome. Awesome to hear. I want to transition to the next question. So what does networking mean to you? Sorry. Yes.

50

V. Rodriguez:

To me, networking means for survival. I truly believe that without relationships in your life, you will not have the opportunity to live your best life. I agree. Networking is the key to a lot of the goals and aspirations and dreams that we have for ourselves. And so for me, without networking, I wouldn't be able to have those things come through the wisdom, and so that's why it's available for me.

Dr. Jairo Borja:

How is it important to your business?

V. Rodriguez:

Networking is very important to my business. Seeds that I planted years ago are what allows us to collect tax today. And that is the results from introducing myself to somebody at the nail salon, or from meeting someone at a conference, networking projects everywhere. And every opportunity that I [inaudible] and my business is [inaudible] client.

Dr. Jairo Borja:

Awesome. Awesome. Thank you. You know, I don't know you too long. I met you just calendar year before when, I know I have respect that you're an amazing networker. So what makes you a great networker?

V. Rodriguez:

I think what makes you a great networker is having back company [inaudible] be able to get into and more time and actually have value and something to it.

Dr. Jairo Borja:

Gotcha, gotcha. You spoke a little bit about the nail salon and your different network, so as whether you're an entrepreneur or whether you're a business owner, what are the different ways that someone could expand their network? Could you provide a couple of examples or an example if possible?

V. Rodriguez:

Probably [inaudible] by connecting with someone anywhere at any time of the day. It doesn't need to be in a traditional sense or feel formal. It doesn't have to be in a conference. That welcome can happen online, that welcome can happen at the grocery store, while you're doing laundry. There really are no badges, all you need is another person that's you're communicating with, and you are networking.

Dr. Jairo Borja:

Yeah. Yeah. Agreed. Agreed, agreed. Why is it important to my readers, whether to volunteer professionally or to volunteer like what you do with the charter schools? Why is it important to serve volunteer professional or volunteer to expand your network?

V. Rodriguez:

Well, A, I think volunteering again because we all have a responsibility to educate and give back. Yeah. And I also believe that reward, that type of humility and gratitude that you extend through volunteering, I think is important professionally because it provides opportunity for you to build your service portfolio in terms of what you do outside of what happens in the office. I think it makes you a Renaissance professional and more marketable. I think it also allows you opportunity for you to expand your network.

V. Rodriguez:

People you normally wouldn't have if you didn't volunteer your time. And again, I feel that we are all here to help each other do better, and so volunteering as a way for us to do that.

Dr. Jairo Borja:

Of course, of course. Great stuff. I added this late in my book actually a few weeks ago. So why is it important to surround yourself with the right people? Whether you know, not just hanging out with the guys in the corner, no disrespect to those guys or gals, but why is it important to surround yourself with the right people?

V. Rodriguez:

It's important because we are all products of our environment. So if you're spending time with people who aren't doing shit, you're going to essentially not do shit either. And so you need to hang around with people who are either in the position you want to be in, can help you get into that position or just provide good energy and provide magic for your soul so that you can keep going when going gets tough or when you feel like giving up.

V. Rodriguez:

So I think there's different types of people, things around yourself. I also think there is value in providing yourself with people who don't do shit, because it would remind you of what will happen if you give up on yourself and you don't continue on your path and working towards whatever it is that you're working for. So I think the majority of your time is spent with people who can influence you in a positive way and really propel you forward. They all do those values. Putting yourself in environments where things aren't necessarily great, so you can always remain humble, and have gratitude when things go well.

Dr. Jairo Borja:

No, exactly. I agree with you a hundred percent. You went to an event a couple of weeks ago, I saw on social media. I wanted to discuss, explain how important A: follow-up is, and B: tell me about your little system. I saw video stories a couple of weeks ago. Can you explain a little bit without giving too many secrets away? Your system as far as what you do post-event as far as collecting business cards and organizing them?

V. Rodriguez:

Yeah, I mean, I can. If you are collecting business cards, you know right on the business card, really key thing that you spoke about in your conversation, but when you follow up you can write those three things so they can remember who you are. Cause I'm sure they're meeting tons of people and so it's important to remind people of the discussions we've had and wellness. We're thinking about those discussions. So that is correct. Another trick is keeping your relationships warm, keeping them in tune with what you have going on. So start a newsletter for yourself or during the holidays just talking with people, bang on these, you know a note of gratitude and thank them for whatever it is, whatever influence they had in your life and thanking them for it.

V. Rodriguez:

That's another way to really take care of your relationships. But, follow up is follow up with where the money is. Follow up is where the magic is, and so you know, just going through that and meeting someone is half the battle. The win that you still need is the follow-up. And that's how you start building real information and following up doesn't mean just one email. It means several times following up and being persistent about it. And so, without the follow-up, you basically wasted your time.

Dr. Jairo Borja:

No, agreed. I think, what is it the average it takes the average person what, seven touchpoints it, or something like that. So have you do one email, yeah, you're not going to get anywhere. Agreed. Agreed. So want to transition real quick. How do you leverage social media, whether it's before an event or an event or post-event? How do you leverage social media? But if you, for an example, as far as for your events, how do you know, what do you, how do you leverage, you're born during and then after social media.

V. Rodriguez:

I use social media, in a number of different ways. Social media is really all about building a community and telling your story and having people follow that story, right? And being relatable and sharing moments when things don't go your way. And being open to being vulnerable because of how you're going to build your community. In terms of how to use social media prior to an event? You let people know what's going on, you let them know what you're doing, how you plan for it. Why are you doing this event? You know, some engaged to outdoor events. You get stories, go live. And then post-event, you give them a recap as to what happened. And again, this is about community. And it's also about you to media as a tool to build a brand for yourself. And use it as a marketing tool that you are aware of what you're doing and on a theme, and you're making things happen when people feel like you are making things happen and you're getting things done, they want to be a part of that.

Dr. Jairo Borja:

Agreed. That was actually my next question, so it leads to my next question. So how could someone use social media or just a website or whatever or in general to kind of build their brand? You actually touched on a little bit, but can you elaborate a little bit more?

V. Rodriguez:

I think the main point to drag home is to be active and be the same. So again, just let people know what you're doing, why you're doing it, let them know the story behind the things that you are doing. You have to get really good at storytelling on social media because there's some noise in this phase. And so you need to be intriguing. And so you need to figure out how to get people to be involved and to, you know, be excited about what it is that you do. And so, you know there's always a lesson in what I post. There's always a reason behind what I post, and we're going to make you feel good, or it's going to light a fire under your ass, so you'll take action.

V. Rodriguez:

That's very much part of my brand, right? I'm helping people become the best version of themselves. So social media has been cool for me in growing my business as well as expanding my network. There are people that I've met over social media such as yourself, who I've been able to build relationships with and business with and get money with. And we'll get our nails done and celebrate holidays together. It is just another way to engage, and you are putting yourself at a disadvantage if you are not using social media, to expand your access, to magnify your brand and or, make money.

Dr. Jairo Borja:

Agreed. I agree 100% yeah, you're right. If it weren't for social media we would have not connected in that... I mentioned the rest of the Facebook group? Any final comments? So just to give you, not a recap but just, you know, just a networking way to success, ten strategies to, you know, expand your network, whether you're an entrepreneur or a business professional. Any final comments, last questions or comments?

V. Rodriguez:

People put a lot of pressure on themselves when it comes to networking. They think that there is a secret formula, but the best advice I can give is be yourself. And if you're dorky, then be your dorky self. Don't try to force anything because you're basically setting yourself up for failure and the obsession to meet as many people and get out there. And so the best way for you to do that and do it consistently is to just be yourself.

Dr. Jairo Borja:

Agreed. Victoria, thank you for your time. I really appreciate you being part of this book and I, and I know you've been a great value to the readers in one way, shape, or form. Thank you. All right. Take care. Thank you so much. Have a great night.

V. Rodriguez:

Alright, bye.

Dr. Jairo Borja:

Alright, thank you. Thanks. Bye-bye.

I had a great interview with Victoria Rodriguez. Though, the coffee shop I was in was extremely loud. However, we got it done. I learned from the interview how Victoria uses social media to tell stories of what she does day in and day out. I also agree with her, following up is where the money is. Yes, it is fun to attend networking events. If you aren't following up though, then what's the point of attending a networking event for business purposes. I hope you enjoyed and learned from the interview.

CHECKLIST POST EVENT & QUIZ

1) Name three things you should do post networking events?
2) Name two things from LinkedIn that should always be on point?
3) What is the difference between short term contacts and long term contacts?
4) Why enter new names of contacts in your CRM and email campaign service?
5) Why use an application such as Camcard to upload contacts on your mobile phone?
6) What are three things you can do with your CRM to help you follow up with clients & prospects?

HOW TO EXPAND YOUR NETWORK BESIDES NETWORKING EVENTS

For the most part, people think networking is just about attending networking events. To expand your network, it is more than just attending events a few times per week. Will you get quantity by attending a few days per week, yes? Will you get quality? Who knows, perhaps? However, for you to expand your network, you should do these three things: volunteer professionally, volunteer for a nonprofit, and join a networking group. After all, participating in any of these will assist in the expansion of your network and, most importantly, your brand. Volunteer professionally. This tactic has assisted me in my career and business. Currently, I am the co-liaison for the ASIS Young Professionals New York City Chapter. Also, I am the Treasurer for Prospanica New Jersey Chapter. In the past, I was on the board for the Hispanic Business Council Scholarship Foundation of New Jersey. Do I get paid for these opportunities? No, I don't. However, thanks to all three organizations I was able to expand my network, have numerous relationships and conduct some great business with great organizations as a result of volunteering professionally. For example, I would attend the International Expo each year for ASIS (now called GSX).

I connected with some high-level people at one of these conferences. As a result, I was able to land some serious contracts for my previous employer. This example is just one example of how volunteering professionally has gotten me the exposure needed to conduct future business with some of the key players in the security profession. Volunteering professionally has helped with my brand because other board members see my work ethic and understand my passion for the mission of each organization. As a result, it is a warm or hot call when I want to set up a sales call for future business.

Another example where volunteering professionally helps me is exposure. I get to human resources professionals and diversity & inclusion specialist volunteering with Prospanica. The different employee resource groups partner with an organization such as Prospanica for diverse programming for its employees. They also partner with Prospanica for recruiting initiatives and events to hire minorities in prominent roles within their organization. Lastly, sponsors partner with Prospanica to provide scholarships for Hispanics for college. Participating with an organization such as Prospanica has given me the exposure to network with key human resources professionals for some of the largest organizations in the state of New Jersey. Moral of the story, join a board.

Volunteer professionally to get the exposure for your brand but also to expand your network. Volunteer nonprofit. Volunteering for a nonprofit will help fulfill the mission of an organization. Nonprofits need assistance in trying to fulfill the mission of an organization but sometimes don't have the resources to fulfill the mission.

Exposure to volunteering at the local shelter, for example, you will have exposure to assisting the staff and its guests. You are building a rapport with the staff of the shelter and, most importantly, assist with its clients. Companies also respect those individuals who give back to the community. Companies and individuals respect those who take time out of their days to give back to the community. For example, I have volunteered at the Hoboken shelter through my previous employer. I loved the opportunity to assist in organizing donated clothes and preparing meals for those who can't afford it. I believe in the law of reciprocity, and it's not just about receiving. It's about giving as well. I am happy to assist those who are less fortunate and giving back to the community. I was happy assisting in fulfilling the mission of the Hoboken shelter, where I volunteered. Volunteering for a nonprofit has assisted with exposure for my brand, as well. It shows that I am not just about maximizing profits. I am about helping others as well. I help out people on LinkedIn all the time, and I may not benefit from it. I believe in the law of reciprocity and giving back. I believe in good karma haha, good karma will come back to me one way, shape or form.

Most importantly, volunteering for a nonprofit will assist in fulfilling the mission of any nonprofit organization. Besides, it will help build the philanthropic side of your organization and your brand in the process. Letip or BNI networking group. By now if you are in business you have heard of Letip or BNI networking group. These are organizations that, by design, have one realtor, one financial services professional, one mortgage broker, one attorney. The purpose of these types of organizations is you meet once a week, and one person highlights their business. Also, referrals are exchanged on a week to week basis. Referrals given are also tracked for data purposes. The advantage of joining a networking group such as Letip or BNI is you are building relationships with these individuals. You have used FORMEA up to this point. You have built trust and credibility for individuals to do business with you.

Now you exchange referrals and not just do business with each other; you can exchange referrals to conduct business with each other's customers. At every meeting, everyone gives a 30 second to 1-minute elevator speech on their business. Also, someone usually has 5-10 minutes for a brief presentation on their product or service. The advantage of a key presentation, such as that is, individuals will learn what your business is all about. Also, individuals in the audience are trying to piece how can your organization fit with their organization. If you are a realtor, mortgage broker, accountant, financial services professional, attorney, I highly recommend you join a networking group such as a Letip or BNI. For example the customer for the accountant will then need financial advice to purchase a home. A mortgage broker can then ensure preapproval to refer then real estate agent who then can refer attorney for contract and closing. That was one example of how all five professionals could benefit from business with their one customer.

In conclusion, I highly recommend joining a networking group. It will help with your business, your brand, and consistent referrals. As an entrepreneur, it is important to maintain prospects in the mill. Don't just depend on straight-up networking events. Volunteer professionally, volunteer for a nonprofit, and join a networking group. It will help build new relationships and, most importantly, expand your network. Lastly, it will help you build your brand, which, when individuals want to do business with you, they will remember you. Trust me, they will remember you. The next chapter is an interview with a friend and colleague of mine, Beth Marmolejos. I think you will enjoy this interview similar to the rest of them. Just some great information overall.

Interview with Beth Marmolejos

My next guest needs no introduction. Beth Marmolejos is currently the Executive Vice President for Prospanica New Jersey Chapter. Previously, Beth was the President of the New York Chapter. Beth is a master networker. Enjoy the interview:

Dr. Jairo Borja:

So just tell everyone who you are and then what boards you're a part of. Because here's the Genesis of the book. So the book is called Networking Your Way to Success: 10 Strategies of How to Expand Your Business for an Entrepreneur, then for networking professionals. So, I consider you a networking master. So with that being said, that's why I had you in my book. So-

Beth Marmolejos:

Thank you.

Dr. Jairo Borja:

No, you're welcome.

Beth Marmolejos:

You are so kind.

Dr. Jairo Borja:

No, any time. Thank you, thank you. So tell everyone who you are, and what you do, and what boards you're a part of. Because I know you, but I know the audience doesn't know you, so.

Beth Marmolejos:

Okay. Can you hear me well?

Dr. Jairo Borja: Yeah, I can hear you well. Yeah, you're good.

Beth Marmolejos:

Okay, because I got myself off the speakerphone. All right. So first and foremost, let me say thank you, Jairo, for thinking of me. I consider you someone who I admire, someone who I get along with. And I am here because I aspire to have your personality. You're very even and calm.

Dr. Jairo Borja:

Thank you. Thank you, thank you. We work well together; that's why.

Beth Marmolejos:

That's right, that's right. So I am Beth Marmolejos, and I am part of the Prospanica New Jersey chapter. And I sit as the Executive Vice President and also former President of the New York chapter. So I've been part of Prospanica, formally known as the National Society of Hispanic with MBA, NSHMBA, since 2011. And I fell in love with your organization, its mission to help Hispanic professionals. And I've been part of, I'm a lifetime member, so I believe in the mission.

Dr. Jairo Borja:

Good. Good, good. All right. And so what does networking mean to you?

Beth Marmolejos:

You know, networking is critical to the success of not only a business professional, but someone who's trying to become an entrepreneur, but to anyone. So I wear many hats. And as an advocate, I will tell you that a lot of the programs that we have started to assist individuals with disabilities or women to progress in their careers through the American Association of Women University, which I belong to, is through connections. So I give an example of the importance of networking with the following an example.

Beth Marmolejos:

So I don't know, and you want to be laughing. But it actually illustrates very well the power of networking. So I don't know if you remember Pretty Woman?

Dr. Jairo Borja:

Yeah, I remember. All right, Julia Roberts, yes.

Beth Marmolejos:

Yes, one of my favorite movies either. And remember that part where she went to the store with tons of money? And she was dressed, and I'm going to use, she was a hooker on the [crosstalk 00:03:56], she was dressed like that. And she put all the money on the table and gave it to the person that was at the store. This was the trendiest store, very fancy in California [inaudible 00:04:08]. And what happened to her?

Beth Marmolejos:

Well, the answer was they did not take her money and actually turned her away. What happened next is the illustration of networking. She went and got Richard Gere, which was the main character. He came back, okay? With his suit and his chauffer, and immediately they opened the door. I know it was another store, but they opened the door, and he asked, "No, we want more help. We need more. This is not enough help for us."

Beth Marmolejos:

So basically because she used his influence and he was in her network, she was able to get what she needed, even though it was denied having the money to buy the merchant.

Dr.. Jairo Borja:
Merchant, wow. That's very powerful.

Beth Marmolejos:

So that's what happens. What happens is in my world, a strong network means more than money. You could have the money, but if you don't have the connections, you don't get far. And that's why networking exists too, right?

Dr. Jairo Borja:

Yeah, yeah, exactly. Agreed, agreed. That's a very powerful story. And that's amazing, that's amazing. So to follow up with that. So what makes you a great network? I know you're all on these boards, but what makes you, you think in your opinion, a great networker per se?

Beth Marmolejos:
Like what's my secret, type of thing?

Dr. Jairo Borja:
I guess, I guess.

70

Beth Marmolejos:

I think a couple of things. I think that when I started my journey into ... Well, a couple of things. I can really take a setback. I did take a class, through a ... And this was the company that I work for most of my career called Medco Health Solutions. They sent me, and they picked women to a class called Women's Unlimited, okay?

Dr. Jairo Borja:

Okay. Okay.

Beth Marmolejos:

And this was 2000, I don't know, I'm just going to say 2008. So once a month, you will go to this class, and they taught me about networking. Okay. Your story, how to craft your message. At that point I didn't really understand what it all meant, but I did take that class, and I think that, that coupled with the fact that I'm very outgoing, as you could tell, makes me really effective.

Beth Marmolejos:

The half Latina, half Italian in me. So I think if I were to summarize what makes me a great network at is I pretty much know what I'm going after because I always have a goal of who I want to talk to, who I need in my network. And I try to keep people, different networks by the way. So more to come on this type of network.

Dr. Jairo Borja:

Yeah, absolutely. So that's a great follow up question. So why should people A, look into other networks, and B, look into volunteering professionally to expand their network?

Beth Marmolejos:

Okay, so-

Dr. Jairo Borja:

I know, it's a lot.

Beth Marmolejos:

No, actually, it isn't.

Dr. Jairo Borja:

Go ahead.

Beth Marmolejos

Okay, so the first question is, why should people have different networks? And I think I mentioned earlier that I wear many hats, right? I am a mother, I'm a business professional, I'm Latina, a mother of a child with autism, and that sort of turned me into an advocate. So even when I go to the gym, I have in each one of those areas, a network that is different from each other. So when I want to create programs for individuals with disability, I'm not going to go to

Prospanica because it has nothing to do with it. I go to the elected officials, right? To open the doors for me.

Beth Marmolejos:

And I'll give you an example. I went to their freeholders in Sussex County, I pitched this idea of a swim team for the county, and they opened the door for a state county check for children with autism, so that's an example. When I'm at the gym, I actually have a group of girls, and most of them are Latina, where we actually through ourselves, talk to each other, we know which teacher is coming, which teacher is good, which isn't bad. What that also brought was help because a couple of them have nonprofits and have helped me with nonprofit work. So that's kind of my [inaudible 00:08:51].

Beth Marmolejos:

And then you know, the Prospanica for all the things. So basically, as a mom, I also have a network of parents that I can reach out to that I know are advocates and will help me with certain things as a mom. So that's why it's important to not just be stuck on a Hispanic network type of type or just for women or just for disability, you have to have it all to be able to accomplish all the goals that you have with the different hat, as an entrepreneur as well.

Dr. Jairo Borja:

Of course, of course. And the second part of the question was, why should individuals volunteer professionally? Whether it's Prospanica, whether it's whatever, National Black MBA, whatever the case.

Beth Marmolejos:

Yeah. So that I will tell you based on my experience, and I'm sorry this phone is ringing behind me. I think that for me, it all started in 2011 where my company at that point, Medco Health Solutions, that I spoke about, that company, they had a takeover, this company called Express Scripts. So you probably know this is a mail-order company. They took over our company. And what we saw just from that was the biggest layoff in the history of the county happened as a result of that takeover.

Beth Marmolejos:

So Ken Espinoza who was with me, part of the diversity and inclusion board in the company, had this brilliant idea of bringing these two organizations, it was the Black MBA and the NSHMBA, the National Society Hispanic with MBA, to offer opportunities for employees that potentially were already laid off, on their way out or we're going to. So to tap into these organizations to get a job.

Beth Marmolejos:

So basically, I did that, and they asked me right away to become within a couple of months, become part of the board. And I started a New Jersey chapter. So that helped me tap into a group that, by the way, my job as an executive, I landed to that relationship. So eventually I put together a healthcare summit at Rutgers University, and I invited the President of Express Scripts, who I know, one of my mentor, and the President of Empire Blue Cross Blue Shield, Brian Griffin.

Beth Marmolejos:

And I went over to him right before we started the event, the Prospanica event, and I said, "Hey, I have two friends that got laid off. Would you have an opportunity for them?" And he turned around and said, "No, but I have an opportunity for you." So again, it opens doors for job opportunities for you, and it helps you also with professional development.

Dr. Jairo Borja:

Absolutely, well said. I couldn't have said it well enough. Now, how important do you think is follow up regarding whether you're at an event? Doesn't matter what kind. I think it's a lost art, in my opinion, especially networking for over a decade. How important is follow up?

Beth Marmolejos:

You know what? I'm guilty, as you are.

Dr. Jairo Borja:

Yes I am.

Beth Marmolejos:

Extremely critical. If you really want to ... First of all, before you [inaudible 00:12:41] of the event and see who the speakers are, right?

Dr. Jairo Borja:

Right.

Beth Marmolejos:

Identify who within, you know the speaker lineup is the person that you want to talk to so that you are clear as to the objective of you attending that event. Get that person's card and then do the follow-up. The follow up could be, "Hey." First of all when you go to someone, you don't go to them and say, "Hey, I'm looking for a job. Can you help me?" It's the biggest turnoff there is. Try to find common ground on things that potentially you like, such as plain goals, which I don't, but people do. And then do the follow-up, "Hey, I was that girl that spoke to you about goals, and I would like to see if you heard of X, Y, and Z," and then establish a conversation from there. I think it's important. I think I need to get better at it. But for the most part I do follow up with the people that are critical to what I'm looking for.

Dr. Jairo Borja:

Good, good. What are your strategies if any at all, do you do set up alarms on your phone? Do you do sticky notes on your computer? Is there anything you do to try to follow up with people for the most part?

Beth Marmolejos:

Well, I have something. It's not like that, but I do have a little delegate. I do. When I go to the events if you get let's say ten cards, right? You try to A, write a note right there, and then that reminds you why that person is important. It could be, or that reminds me of who that was. Like she had a dog, and you know that you spoke about the dog and you know, "Okay, I know who she is." But two, if it's important, I actually take the corner of the car, and I fold it into a triangle. That tells me that that's an important person, and I need to potentially follow up with that person.

Dr. Jairo Borja:

Oh, that's interesting. I've never heard of that. That's pretty cool.

Beth Marmolejos:

Yeah. It's different. It works.

Dr. Jairo Borja:

It works, though, whatever works, right?

Beth Marmolejos:
Yeah.

Dr. Jairo Borja:

So now I'll transition over into the last question is a big question. So what is the best way to leverage social media, whether it's pre-event or post-event? You see it more and more. You and I are very good at that, but I mean, for the average person, what do you think is the best way to leverage social media pre and post-event?

Beth Marmolejos:

I think if I'm capturing the gist of the question, the best way, the way that I do, I don't use social media at all to post about social things that I do. Like, "Ah, I'm at a restaurant drinking a beer." I always try to have a topic of what I'm trying to promote for my brand. And if you go to my posts, they're all similar. You won't find me like at a pool jumping from a cable or something. It's always about, really, it's about I stick to the topics of advocacy, professional development, and community.

Beth Marmolejos:

So I use social media to get people to either volunteer, donate to a cause, attend an event. And people take me seriously. When I text somebody, they know that it's about something that is of interest. It's not about a party where everybody's going to get drunk or something. You know? So I leverage to help promote the things that part of. For example, the PAC event that we have coming. Because I know that people are asking me, "Hey, do you know where there are job opportunities?" And so you know, I right away post things that could help other people one way or the other.

Dr. Jairo Borja:

Right. And how would you leverage that post-event? I guess showing pictures of results?

Beth Marmolejos:

Yeah. It's more for me, if it's a professional type of event like the Prospanicas, I try to post-event put, "Hey, this was a successful event," to show that we have power. And thank the speakers or their organization that hosted the event. So that's how I use it in that scenario. If it's a gala, then I pretty much try to show pictures with and values like the Dominican Gala. Picture with the girls that were selected. Well, the concerts with the crowns and the presenting of the parade, and I say, "Hey, we're doing this to preserve the culture. Thanks to the elected officials that attended," to show that are paying attention to whether they're supporting our community. And to

www.BorjaConsultingGroup.com

79

show also the caliber of what we're doing. Right? It's an event that is very classy and elegant. Right?

Dr. Jairo Borja:

Right. Of course, of course. Yeah, it all depends on post-event.

Beth Marmolejos:

Exactly.

Dr. Jairo Borja:

All right, so yeah. You have any final comments? This is good. It was real simple, straight to the point. Any final comments to the people reading this book regarding networking?

Beth Marmolejos:

The first step to becoming a network ninja savvy. So kudos to them. Thank you. And to you, I'm saying the sky's not even the limit for you. It's great that you're doing this, and I know you're doing this for the purpose of helping others.

Dr. Jairo Borja:

Exactly. Exactly. Thank you, Beth. Thank you so much. Thank you. I really appreciate it. Thank you.

I learned so much from the interview with Beth. Beth has various networks from the boards she participates in, to who she works out with. I learned that Beth is strategic of what she posts on social media. Beth understands the importance of building your brand. In addition, Beth uses social media to get people to donate for a great cause or to promote upcoming events. I hope you learned a thing or two about expanding your networking from this great interview.

Leveraging Social Media and Social Media Management

Social media management so important, especially in today's business. Especially if you are an entrepreneur, I use LinkedIn, Twitter, Instagram, and Facebook. In the beginning, I would post items separately on each platform. Now I use Hootsuite. Hootsuite is great because it allows me to post one time and it will go out all of my social media platforms. The advantage of that is that I am consistent with my message and not everyone uses all four social media platforms. I can reach as many people as possible this way. I highly recommend using social media management software. One advantage is you can manage customer service more efficiently. Any area of improvement comment or concern you can manage that by using a social media management system. Any concerns from customers that voice their opinion via social media, you can address right away, and it will not sit unaddressed which can hurt your brand. Another advantage of Hootsuite is you can schedule posts. Depending on the brand, timing is everything. Scheduling posts allows for you as the entrepreneur to focus on other aspects of the business and know that your social media post is scheduled to be posted at a later date. You can also view analytic data of who is viewing your posts, from which site and from which locations. This tactic is so important in knowing your audience when it comes to marketing your product or service.

Facebook had 2.32 billion users in 2018. 95% of adults ages 18-34 are most likely following a social media brand via social networking. I will give you one more mind-blowing statistic the active number of global mobile social media users is 3.3 billion global equaling 42% penetration (Statista, 2019). If you aren't good with social media or your website, hire a professional to run this part of your business. As an entrepreneur, your biggest key to your success is closing deals and continue to prospect for clients, filling the funnel. If you are not prospecting, it will be challenging for you to stay in business.

In conclusion, using a social media management tool such as Hootsuite is so important for your business. You want to have a clear and consistent message throughout all of your social media platforms. You will be able to manage your network and your posts much simpler. You can schedule posts so you can focus on closing deals and prospecting as an entrepreneur.

Final Checklist & Quiz

1. Name three ways you can expand your business besides networking events?
2. How can using social media management software help you with your business?
3. Why is volunteering Professionally so important to your brand and network?
4. How can volunteer at a nonprofit help your network and brand?
5. What are the advantages of joining a networking group?
6. How many people have used Facebook in 2018?

Surround Yourself with Successful People

Writing this book, I did not think of this originally. However, it is so important to watch who are you surrounded with. For example, I grew up in Corona, Queens, NY. Yes, we are the only borough that lists the neighborhood along with the borough. We are proud of where we come from; that is why. However, for me to expand my network, I had to expand out of Corona, Queens, NY. That is why I went to undergrad, graduate school and eventually graduate school again for my doctorate. Each one of those networks at each school has made me elevate my game. I see others with successful businesses, and I want to do the same. However, individuals make several mistakes in who they surround themselves with.

The first mistake, you stay in your neighborhood. What do I mean by that? Even after your respective schoolings, you may work in the city. However, you do not look to expand your network. You stick with your friends in your neighborhood. There is nothing wrong with that. However, if you want to succeed in your job or your business, you have to expand out of your network. You want to compete with not just the individuals in your neighborhood. However, you want to compete with individuals in your borough or county. By looking to expand your network, you meet new people that are also just as successful or perhaps even more. Surrounding yourself with successful people makes you want to elevate your own game, and just by interacting with other networks outside of your own, it makes you a better person. As a person, you want to step up your game, your network, and take actions such as professional development, additional courses, additional degrees, additional programs for you to expand your network. That is how you step it up; that is how you elevate your game.

The second mistake, you don't volunteer professionally. I mentioned this earlier in the book. If you volunteer professionally for an organization, you surround yourself with other successful individuals in your profession. Although you volunteer and have the same vision and mission for the nonprofit, as professionals you both want to learn from each other. You learn what has worked for you and made you successful in your everyday business. Then you implement what you learned from the other professionals and see if it works for your everyday business. As an entrepreneur and business owner, it is important to learn new things and implement different strategies to have your business constantly expanding. Surround yourself and your network with other professionals to elevate your game.

The last mistake, you hang out with the wrong crowd. If you hang out with four idiots, you are going to be the fifth idiot. As a business professional, please be careful who you surround yourself with. You have an image; you have a brand. If you know that if you get into that car or that club and you know bad things can happen, avoid it by not going. Just say no. Your image, your business imagine yourself as being watched 24 hours a day for seven days per week. If you know that certain people have certain things that go against your image, your brand, and if you know that one mistake or one incident can taint that image or brand, make the educated decision of just not getting into that car or going to that club. As a business owner and coach, I advise my clients always to be mindful of what they post on social media as well. You don't want to be posting drunk pictures of yourself or pictures and videos of you doing shots. If you are promoting an alcohol beverage, more power to you, however, if you want to be taken seriously and want customers to trust you with your product or service, you should not be posting inappropriate photos and videos. Posting these inappropriate photos and videos can hurt your brand.

In conclusion, be careful of who you surround yourself with, make those educated decisions when going out during the weekend. Also, make those educated decisions before posting photos and videos on social media. Please be mindful that what you post on social media is a representation of your business and, most importantly, you. It is important to be mindful of who you surround yourself with. It is important to expand outside of your neighborhood. There is so much to see in the county, in the state, in the country, in the world. The further you expand, the more different ideas you can see, the more successful professionals in your industry you can meet. Another mistake people make is they don't volunteer professionally. Eat, sleep, work, repeat. Business professionals don't always think of spending the extra time volunteering professionally for a nonprofit to achieve the mission and vision of the nonprofit. But you must, in the process, connect with different business professionals and elevate your game to be as successful if not more successful in being the best at what you do. Lastly, you may hang out with the wrong crowd and make some bad decisions if you aren't mindful of how you post on social media. You don't realize that what you post on social media is a representation of your brand and you. It is important to make educated decisions and choosing who you hang out with — also, making educated decisions when posting those videos or photos from the club on social media. I think you will love my next interview with Jocelyn Russo. A great friend and my realtor.

Interview with Jocelyn Russo

I've known Jocelyn for over 6 to 7 years. I've seen her grow her real estate practice. I consider Jocelyn an excellent networker. I hope you enjoy this interview and learn from Jocelyn her techniques and what makes her successful. Enjoy:

Dr. Jairo Borja:

I know who you are, but tell everyone for the sake of the book who you are and what you do and what boards you're on.

Jocelyn Russo:

I am Jocelyn Russo, and my specialty is real estate and helping people, whether they are a first time home buyer, they were renting, and they're looking to buy, or they are a move-up homeowner, meaning they were in a smaller home and now they've outgrown that and they want to transition to a bigger home. I also work with people who are downsizing a lot. I help with the estate sale process. I can help with moving somebody into a 55 or older community or moving out of state. I'm really big on relocating people in and out of New Jersey. The boards that I am on, I am on the North Central Jersey Board of Realtors, which is the largest board of realtors in the state. We are considered a mega board.

Jocelyn Russo:

I am the past president of YPN, which is Young Professionals Network. I've done a lot of volunteer work with them for … They have a Thanksgiving turkey drive. They have another event called Realtor Care Day, where they take two or three distressed homes that are in Northern New Jersey, and we will do like an exterior semi, not renovation, but like if it needs painting and gardening and stuff like that, to a house. I also volunteered with that. I'm pretty big with the board. I also used to be part of the North Jersey Chamber of Commerce. I'm the past ambassador for them, but those are probably the two main boards that I've been a part of.

Dr. Jairo Borja:

That's great. That's great to hear. I appreciate it. Now moving onto the next question, so what does networking mean to you?

Jocelyn Russo:

Networking means to me is connecting, connecting people who can utilize someone's service, or you think it would be just a good business to business connection, but I really think networking is connecting. I love when I meet somebody that is looking for a certain type of person that owns a certain type of company, and I have that person, and I take person A and person B, put them together, and it creates like a beautiful flower. That, to me, is so rewarding because I'm helping two people that don't know each other. I probably know both of them, and I made that connection. That, to me, is networking.

Dr. Jairo Borja:

That's great. That's awesome. That's awesome. I want to ask another question. What makes you a great networker you think, more about the connecting, or is there anything else you want to elaborate on that?

Jocelyn Russo:

What makes me a great networker is I am very influential, I think, with networking. I want to really make sure when I go to an event or if I'm even doing an event myself, I'm very interactive. I'm always prepared. I have business cards. I think it's really important that when you're part of any kind of networking, you're prepared and you have high energy. You're talking to people. You're not just sitting in a corner on your phone and expecting to meet people.

Jocelyn Russo:

This past weekend I just did two events. I had our Montclair sidewalk sale. We had a table outside, and we literally talked to everybody who walked by. Every person that walked by, I said, "Hello, how are you? Are you thinking of moving in the next couple of months?" I gave them a gift. We gave them a gift bag. I was so interactive, and I got to meet so many people and network with so many great people. If I just stood there and I was just on my phone the whole time or wasn't interactive then I wasn't going to meet anybody.

Dr. Jairo Borja:

Of course.

Jocelyn Russo:

I think it's really interaction and being prepared and having really good energy.

Dr. Jairo Borja:

That's great. That's great. Do you have any techniques as far as … We'll talk about follow up in a few minutes, but any techniques you do with your business cards? Do you write, I don't know, a note or is there any … What do you do to remember each person?

Jocelyn Russo:

Yeah. Usually we'll write a little something on their card. Yeah.

Dr. Jairo Borja:

Okay, cool.

Jocelyn Russo:

What we spoke about or if I have to send them something or if we put a meeting, I'll put it in my calendar. I usually do some type of note on their card.

Dr. Jairo Borja:

Yep. I do the same thing, because I'm not going to remember 50, 100 people I met at an event. I got to do something, whether it's something they wore or something they said or they're a fan of sports or whatever it is. I always write it down, and afterwards I can [crosstalk 00:07:43] refer back to it.

Jocelyn Russo:

A little trick that I think is really important is to do it right away, whether it be the day of or the next morning, because it's fresh in your brain. If you put a bunch of business cards, and then a week later you try to remember them, it's more difficult.

Dr. Jairo Borja:

Yep. Agreed. Agreed. Agreed. You are the genesis of the reason why I added to my book. I wanted to get into that as well. Regarding surrounding yourself, why is it important to surround yourself with other successful people, whether it's in your field or outside your field? Why do you think that's so important?

Jocelyn Russo:

I think it's really important because it makes you level up. It's going to put you at a higher standard. If you are surrounding yourself with smart people who are educated, they're forward-thinking, they have a growth mindset, all that stuff, I mean, you naturally reflect that. It's interesting because I have some really amazing friends in the real estate industry that are not even in my area. I have one in New York, one in Florida, just different areas of the country. I talk to them, and I'm seeing things that they're doing, and it's like, "Wow, I need to level up. I need to get my standard's higher." Then I'll talk to them, and they'll motivate me more. They'll say, "Jocelyn, you have to do this, this and this." I'm like, "Oh my God, you're right."

Jocelyn Russo:

It almost brings that light bulb effect to your brain because someone else is doing it, somebody else is benefiting from it. They're successful from it. Now it's just teaching you. I mean, who you surround yourself with is a reflection of yourself. If you really want to be a better person in life and in business, you have to surround yourself with better people.

Dr. Jairo Borja:

Yeah, I agree. I agree 100%. I know we discussed this a little bit before when we were together a couple of weeks ago, but yeah, I absolutely agree. It levels up your game, and it wants you to be on your toes. Whether it's in your industry or just in general, you want people to perceive you as a professional in your respective field, for sure.

Jocelyn Russo:

Yeah, absolutely.

Dr. Jairo Borja:

Yeah. Yeah. Speaking of surrounding yourself, so as far as from a networking standpoint, so why should people, you think, should look into volunteering professionally or just even just volunteering just to kind of like expand their network? Why do you think is that a great suggestion?

Jocelyn Russo:

Well, I think volunteering puts a different level of service out there for you as an individual.

Dr. Jairo Borja:

Of course. Sure.

Jocelyn Russo:

I mean, as you know, like I had interns work for me. In a way, that's like volunteering my time.

Dr. Jairo Borja:

Yep, of course.

Jocelyn Russo:

Teach them and to get them with the mindset of business and all that stuff. I think when you volunteer, it's just like the next wave of working, but you're doing it for like the benefit of somebody else.

Dr. Jairo Borja:

Right.

Jocelyn Russo:

You're putting somebody else before you. I think when you volunteer your time, you're not getting paid for it, but it's an experience that you're putting under your belt and it's important to do. I need to volunteer even more. My goal is to volunteer like once a month doing something, whether it's ... I used to volunteer for the Montclair Art Museum. I was literally a door greeter and I would just say, "Hey, welcome to the museum." People would come up to me and they would be like, "Thank you so much for your smile. You made my day." I'm like, "Well, thank you."

Dr. Jairo Borja:

That's great.

Jocelyn Russo:

I was around a positive environment and met some really nice people, and it allows you to just grow in a different way. I think volunteering is really important.

Dr. Jairo Borja:

That's awesome. Just to elaborate on that, so I know NAHREP, National Association for Hispanic Real Estate Professionals, is big in real estate. Prospanica is big for Hispanic professionals. From a professional development standpoint, do you think people should look into getting into those organizations, whether it's for networking or professional development or both? What's your opinion on that?

Jocelyn Russo:

Well actually for not ... I think it's important for both, for professional development and for networking.

For NAHREP specifically, I don't know if you knew this, but I just won the 2019 top 250 realtors in the country.

Dr. Jairo Borja:

I did not know that. Congratulations. Awesome. I didn't know that.

Jocelyn Russo:

Thank you. Yeah.

Dr. Jairo Borja:

Awesome.

Jocelyn Russo:

For NAHREP, for my half Puerto Rican.

Dr. Jairo Borja:

Half Puerto Rican, that's awesome.

Jocelyn Russo:

No, it's really ... It's an amazing accomplishment. I mean, 250 out of a million realtors, that's like huge.

Dr. Jairo Borja:

Of course.

Jocelyn Russo:

That's the first thing. Then the second thing, because I won that, NAHREP asked me to speak on a panel.

Dr. Jairo Borja:

Right.

Jocelyn Russo:

I spoke on a panel maybe in March, I believe, March of 2019. In that panel they asked me about teams. They asked me about what I do on my daily routine, what I do for business. I was giving pretty much all my secrets, everything I do, to a group of about a 100, 150 people, NAHREP members. I didn't have to do that. I sat there and I just told everybody what I do. People were like taking notes, writing down, asking me questions. I mean, they literally were so grateful that I was sharing this information with them because some people were a brand new agent, some people were a really seasoned agent that just needed that boost of confidence or motivation or whatever.

Dr. Jairo Borja:

Exactly.

Jocelyn Russo:

I gave it to two totally separate people, which was so cool. During the panel I was up there with like five other realtors that were really doing well. One of the guys up there was 22 years old and he was doing some stuff that I don't do.

Dr. Jairo Borja:

Right.

Jocelyn Russo:

I was like, "Wow, this kid motivated me."

Dr. Jairo Borja:

Exactly.

Jocelyn Russo:

With volunteering, yes, networking is great, which I think it's a huge part of it, but the professional development that you could give to people and people will do to you, that's just ... That's amazing.

Dr. Jairo Borja:

Awesome. Awesome. That's awesome to hear. How important do you think is follow up, whether you ... For example, you did that panel. You did the event. Let's say people got back to you. Whether it's professional development or whether they're looking for homes or at any event, how important is follow up to you, whether you reply to people within a day or two days? How important is that to you?

Jocelyn Russo:

I think it's extremely, extremely important. What I'm doing is I'm just following up via social media because nowadays that's just where everybody is. When I was on the NAHREP panel, I got like 20 to 30 new followers on Instagram.

Dr. Jairo Borja:

Wow.

Jocelyn Russo:

I followed everybody back, and now we're following each other. That's the way kind of everyone's going between Instagram, Facebook, LinkedIn. I really like ... I'm also a part of ... Oh, I forgot to mention this. I'm also part of Commerce In Industry. I think I told you about that group.

Dr. Jairo Borja:

Yeah, you told me, yep. Yeah, that's right. Yes, you did.

Jocelyn Russo:

I always go to their women's breakfast they have once a quarter. They have like a women's entrepreneur type of group that I really think is important to go to. Every time that they have an event they give you an Excel spreadsheet of every person that went there. I take that Excel spreadsheet, I contact everybody on LinkedIn and send them a message, "Hey, it was great to meet you," and that's my follow up. I've gotten so much great feedback. "Hey, it was great to meet you too. The speaker was so great, blah, blah, blah, blah, blah." Again, it just makes that connection.

Dr. Jairo Borja:

Exactly.

Jocelyn Russo:

Funny enough, I met an attorney, a woman attorney that does bankruptcy. Her office is right across the street from mine.

Dr. Jairo Borja:

Oh wow.

Jocelyn Russo:

We met at that breakfast, and she emails me that we needed to meet for lunch. I emailed her back and said, "Great. Thursday or Friday I'm free, blah, blah,

blah." She never responded. Next week, I emailed her again. "Hey, do you want to get that lunch?" Never responded.

Dr. Jairo Borja:

Wow.

Jocelyn Russo:

Now, the follow up went out the window.

Dr. Jairo Borja:

Exactly.

Jocelyn Russo:

I'm kind of disappointed because your follow up is the reflection of how you do business, in my opinion.

Dr. Jairo Borja:

Absolutely, absolutely. Absolutely, totally agree. I agree with you. That's a reflection. That's your reputation, you know what I mean? I agree with you.

Jocelyn Russo:

Right.

Dr. Jairo Borja:

I agree with you 100%.

Jocelyn Russo:

Now that she never answered me for lunch, she just left me hanging, am I really going to refer her business?

Dr. Jairo Borja:

Probably not. Exactly. Exactly. You touched a little bit on a little bit on social media. I'll get into that. What's the best way to leverage social media, whether it's pre-event or post-event? What do you think is the best way to leverage social media? I know you do it very well, but what do you think is your opinion, the best way to leverage it? If you have an event, for example, what's the best way to leverage social media? Obviously promoting it, getting people there, and then also post-event, why is it important to kind of post stuff regarding post-event as well?

Jocelyn Russo:

Well, I think there's one step that is missed there. It's pre, during and post.

Dr. Jairo Borja:

Yes. Yeah, pre, during ... That's what I meant, pre, during and post. Yeah.

Jocelyn Russo:

Yeah. I think that you'll need to do all three of

them. You're asking which one's the most important or how to leverage all three?

Dr. Jairo Borja:

How to leverage all three.

Jocelyn Russo:

I will do really just post ... I mean, I'm big on stories because a lot of people like to watch them. Going live is another way to leverage. Pre, "Hey, I'm at this breakfast, blah, blah, blah." Then while I'm there, doing a quick video. I'm really big on video. I think the best way to leverage social media is utilizing video, whether it be through a story or through a post, whatever it is, but I think people are more engaged when you're talking to them versus just a picture.

Dr. Jairo Borja:

Exactly.

Jocelyn Russo:

Then post-event like, "Oh my gosh, I met five people that want to sell their house with me. This is such a great event. If you're looking to be involved in women's business, let me know." Then you're kind of engaging. I think that I would say leveraging is video and really like while you're there at the event to kind of get your friends and followers there with you, and then the success strategy of like engaging with them because of the success that you've got.

Dr. Jairo Borja:

All right. Final question or next to final question, what's the best way do you think to brand yourself to leverage networking, if that question makes sense?

Jocelyn Russo:

Say it one more time.

Dr. Jairo Borja:

What's the best way to brand yourself to leverage your network, do you think, for networking purposes?

Jocelyn Russo:

When I go to a networking event, I usually wear my name tag. That's huge because people will, one, remember me, two, recognize my name. Do you know how many times people will look at my name tag and they'll say, "Jocelyn Russo, I've heard your name before. I've seen you before." I won't even tell them my name or even introduce myself. That is huge.

Dr. Jairo Borja:

Right.

Jocelyn Russo:

Always being prepared with business cards. I mean, you want to have a stack of business cards and make sure that when you're giving it to somebody, you're having a conversation because they're going to remember you and you're going to remember them.

Jocelyn Russo:

I would say your brand is you, no matter what industry that you're in. Make it known. You're the person. You've got your name ... I mean, I wear name tags for my industry. A lot of industries don't, but so many people look at my name tag and will put marketing together for ... Another thing, people will look at my business card, see my picture, and they'll say, "I've seen your picture before. You mailed something to my house, haven't you?" It happened on Sunday. An older woman said that to me. I've never mailed anything to her house, but she swears she has all my stuff that I've ever sent [inaudible 00:00:21:11]. I was like, "Sounds good."

Dr. Jairo Borja:

That's funny. That's funny. Any final thoughts for entrepreneurs or even networking or business professionals reading this book, for the final advice, final comments for either or, either the entrepreneur or the professional trying to expand their network more?

Jocelyn Russo:

I would say to always be growing, because if you're not growing, you're dead. I feel like there's never a plateau in any profession you're in, whether it's whatever industry or even just networking, you can always grow. You can always better yourself, even to your elevator pitch of what you're saying when you're networking. I mean, you have 30 seconds to wow somebody. Do you work on that frequently? What do you say? What points do you really cover? I would just say that always better yourself, practice and grow within your mindset and yourself in general.

Dr. Jairo Borja:

Well, Jocelyn, thank you so much. Our time is just about done, but I really appreciate your contributions to the book and your advice and your expertise and hopefully people learn from the book, from reading the book. I really appreciate your time. Thank you so much.

Jocelyn Russo:

All right. Absolutely, anytime. I'll talk to you soon.

Dr. Jairo Borja:

Talk to you soon. All right. Take care. Thank you so much.

Jocelyn Russo:

Okay, take care. You're welcome. Bye-bye.

Dr. Jairo Borja:

All right, thanks. Thanks. Thank you. Thank you. Bye-bye.

I loved my interview with Jocelyn. I love how she is leveraging social media and using video in her marketing of herself and promoting the different open houses. All of my participants stress the importance of networking and building relationships. Most importantly, making connections with your clients and prospects. I hope you enjoyed the interview and learned from Jocelyn.

Affiliate Marketing

Working as a Director of Business Development for six years and now as an owner of my own consulting company, I have learned that partnerships are one of the biggest strengths for you to be successful whether you work for a company or yourself. Partnerships are so important in business today. For me, thus far as a business owner, I credit my success to the partnerships I have developed over the past decade. Although predominantly in the world of Justice Studies, I have connected well with entrepreneurs over the years that wanted to give a college student a chance at working for an entrepreneur. In the process, the intern would expedite the day to day activities of the entrepreneur. The next paragraph will provide several examples of how partnerships have made me successful over the years.

One example is in my new role as an entrepreneur and business owner. I am grateful that I have been able to aspire and inspire new entrepreneurs by taking a leap of faith and at least piloting the business part-time to start. One of my former coworkers needed some assistance and advice during the formation of her new business. As a coach and consultant, I was more than happy to oblige. Through our conversation, she was able to form her business and begin her services while still being employed with her current employer. In exchange, I am going to be one of her first clients on the event planning side. She is going to help me create some events that will give my consulting company some exposure but also expose her to her target market as well to expand her client portfolio. Collaborating and partnering with her is a win-win for both of us. For me, I can use her services and create events together to expand my reach to be able to assist people as much as possible. For her, she can gain experience, gain exposure and expand her reach of collaborating with more entrepreneurs to be future clients.

Another example is in my old role as Director of Business Development in higher education for a college. I was able to connect with various professionals in the legal and security field and assist these organizations in finding the best talent for their internship program. I also assist these legal and security field organizations fill positions with their respective organizations. The great thing about the internship program is that the program you can try before you buy. What do I mean by that? Students enrolled in the internship program had to do a certain number of hours for the semester. Supervisors and business owners can see the work ethic of these interns. Several examples are interns working on important projects that are crucial for the department or business of the company. Group dynamics and determining if the intern gets along with the other employees are so important in business. The intern has to fit with the vision of the department. Also, the intern has to fit with the overall organization or business. Partnerships were so important for me. I needed these partnerships to not only assist the organizations, and I needed these partnerships to assist the students as well.

For my business Borja Consulting Group, partnerships are crucial to the success of my business. I am collaborating with several businesses on various projects. I am partnering with several other business owners for several reasons. First, we are stronger together — no reason why we should be working in silos if we are targeting the same demographic and customer. We should work together as partners and 50% of something better than 100% of nothing. Besides, as entrepreneurs, we can collaborate and leverage each other's strengths. For example, I have a great network. My friend is a business owner but has a project management background. I know another business owner who owns a restaurant. My friend knows someone who owns a media company. Why not work together so that we can all have some business together as supposed to do a one-off and a catering event, why not collaborate as a team and have ongoing business with each other. The event can get promoted, catered, organized to my established network.

The second reason, partnerships are great because you can consider them extensions or arms of your own business. For example, you may have an accounting service as part of your everyday business. If you were to collaborate with a CPA, you could refer your current clients to your CPA contact. In exchange let's say you are an attorney and specialize in wills. Once you complete wills for your clients, you can say, let me introduce you to my CPA who can assist you in ensuring you are set from a tax standpoint. Why have the CPA and attorney work in silos? Instead, collaborate and work as a team to prospect new clients. This way, both the attorney and CPA's client will benefit from both of your services. As I always like to say "Working smarter, not harder!"

A third reason is referrals, which I now know as an entrepreneur how important referrals in general are. "Working smarter not harder!" Instead of cold calling all day. Why not ask your current client for 4-5 referrals per person. Hey listen, who can you introduce me to that can benefit from the same services I just provided you. For example, if you did that for four of your current clients per week, that would be sixteen referrals per week. It is much easier to contact 16 warm calls and referrals as opposed to cold calls. My suggestion is always to have your client provide some introduction and heads up saying that hey, I gave your number to XYZ, he or she is going to be calling you later today. As an entrepreneur, you are creating partnerships with your clients, and it is far more than just a product or service provided to your clients. In essence, you are creating a full-fledged partnership with your clients and leveraging them for more introduction.

The final reason, I believe in reciprocity. If you want to succeed in any business, reciprocity has to exist. What do I mean? It is not just about me, me, me. It is not just about referrals received but referrals given. As an entrepreneur, you should try to become not just great at obtaining referrals; you should try to become a resource for individuals. Whenever, anyone has a question about who do I contact if I want to buy a house, buy a car, invest in the market, you want individuals to think of you to make those connections. For example, recently someone needed an introduction for a job on LinkedIn. Although I am no longer in the recruiting space, I was able to make an introduction of a candidate to a recruiter. That person contacted me recently and notified me that she got the job last week. That made my day. I love to help people, and for this reason, individuals come to me when they need help. I may not have all the answers however, through my established network, someone may have the answer. Don't just think about yourself, think about others and assist others when you can.

Affiliate Marketing, I know that is the title of this chapter. What is it? Why did I speak about my experiences and working smarter, not harder? Why did I get into speaking about referrals? We understand that many of us have more than one stream of income. Most of us have our employer and then have either a side business or side hustle or have a part-time job. Something that I heard about in the last few years is affiliate marketing. My definition of affiliate marketing is referring a client to someone and obtaining a referral fee for referring that client. It is a win-win for both parties. For you by referring a client, the organization is taking advantage of your network, but that is ok, you are getting paid a referral fee for basically an introduction and being the bridge and making the connection for both parties. For the organization obtaining the referral, the organization is grateful because the organization would not have obtained that client if it wasn't for you. For the client, they trust you, and your client is being serviced by the organization you referred to them too. It is a win-win for everyone. As an entrepreneur, consider assisting your network even more by becoming a resource and affiliate marketer for organizations you can partner with. You create an extra stream of income by becoming an affiliate marketer for an organization. As an entrepreneur especially in the beginning, partnerships are important. So why not leverage your network, become a resource to your network and get paid in the process. As an entrepreneur, you make the introduction, and if the organization closes the deal with your referral you get a referral fee. Easy as 1-2-3.

This book is about networking and the various strategies used to build your network. Reciprocity in networking is important. It is not just about you but about your network. As an entrepreneur, you should not just bank on one deal or one stream of income. You should have several streams of income so that if it doesn't work with one stream of income this week or month, you have other streams of income to rely on. What easier way to set that up than with affiliate marketing? I hope you understand the importance of partnerships and how you can leverage them to become an affiliate marketer.

Your Board of Directors

For a board of directors, there is usually a chairman or chairperson. Sometimes that chairperson or chairman is the President of the organization as well. Sometimes, the President and Chairperson are separate. Also, you have sometimes had an emeritus who has stepped down from their role as president, is still involved in the organization, and assisting through the transition to the new president. You also have other professionals from different industries on the board. The purpose of that is to provide objectively different opinions and fresh perspectives and ideas to the organization they serve.

I mention this because you should create your board of directors. You are the chairman of your board. What do I mean by that? For example, I have a mentor that I always contact every couple of weeks. I use this mentor as an accountability partner. I have used this mentor to vent when frustrated with certain situations. We have bounced around different ideas and has given me some great advice when needed. He is my emeritus; he is my mentor. I also have a CPA I partner with, and whenever I have any questions or need any assistance, I rely on my CPA for questions for different situations.

Another example is a realtor I partner with. If my clients have any questions about different scenarios in real estate, and I don't have the answers, I can always rely on my realtor to answer any questions. Also, if any of my clients want to get referred to a realtor, I always keep my realtor in mind and refer anyone I know that is looking for a new home to my realtor.

My recommendation as a business owner and entrepreneur is to have your board of directors. Even if you don't meet in person, connect with your board of directors online. If you can connect with them in person even better, as a business owner and entrepreneur, you should have an attorney, realtor, accountant, financial adviser, mortgage broker, a small business banker. It is what I discussed earlier in the book, working smarter, not harder. You should be able to assist one client, and your board of directors should also be able to assist your client. Your client should be able to have a conversation with each member of your board.

For example, if you have a client that requires purchasing a home. The realtor refers the client to the mortgage broker. The mortgage broker can ensure that the person is preapproved. Then the client can work with the realtor to find a home. Once the client finds a home, makes an offer, goes review with an attorney. A realtor can refer to attorney on your board of directors. Once contract is approved, work with mortgage broker on closing. Also, have an inspector on your board of directors as well, or the realtor can refer your client as well. Once the home is great, you can go to closing. Once the home is closed on, the realtor recommends connecting with a financial adviser for financial planning and insurance for the home. A financial planner can refer a client to attorney to ensure from a tax standpoint; client is up to date. Especially if client is a business owner, ensures that everything is up to date from a tax standpoint. Now once the home is closed and the business owner wants to expand business, you can refer client to a small business banker. The small business banker will suggest options whether he or she can obtain a business credit card or perhaps even obtain a small business loan to expand their business.

In conclusion, this is why as a business owner, you should build and be the chairperson of your board of directors. As you can see from my example, one client can have an interaction with a realtor, accountant, financial advisor, attorney, mortgage broker, and small business banker. I mentioned this earlier in my book, and it is about working smarter, not harder. It is about partnerships with your board of directors to assist your clients. Instead of working in silos and prospecting separately, work together, assist the client, and everyone can benefit from working with the client.

Similar to a traditional board of directors, the chairperson should communicate changes in the business. In a traditional board of directors, board members are informed of how business is doing. Sometimes, the board of directors is active in the sense that they provide suggestions when needed at meetings. Also, board members act as ambassadors to the company. Just as a traditional board of directors, think of this same mindset for your board of directors. Always keep your board informed of what you are doing in your business. Did you obtain a new product or service? Did you obtain a substantial client? What are the latest trends in your industry or market? It is important just as in a traditional board of directors, to maintain your board of directors informed with the latest news on your business.

For example, if you notify your board of a new product or service, the board members can act as ambassadors of your product or service to their clients. This way, your board members can refer you, clients. Your board members understand that if they refer clients to you, eventually, that client will need the services of the other members of the board of directors. That is why it is important to constantly communicate with your board members. All it takes is for your board members to be in your email campaign and CRM. At a minimum of once per month, you should be sending out an email to your clients of the latest news in your industry and market.

This email serves as not just added value to your clients but also added value to your board of directors. Your board of directors wants to know that they can rely on you when they have a question, for support and, for servicing clients of other members of the board of directors. From a social media standpoint, if you don't have the time to manage your social media as a business, delegate to a member of your team. If you can't delegate, automate. You can use software such as Hootsuite to post your social media consistent throughout all the major platforms. This way you can have a consistent message not just to your clients but prospects and your board members as well. Between using email campaigns through your CRM and being consistent on social media, your board members will be informed of your latest product, services, and trends in your industry. This way your board can advocate for you and when recommending your product or service to their clients.

In conclusion, I hope you understand the concept of having your board of directors as a business owner. I hope you understand that I provided several examples of comparing a traditional board of directors to your board of directors. Also, understand the importance of working smarter in referring clients to each other. Understanding the process of having one client have conversations with each member of your board of directors. That is working smarter, that is how everyone stays in business, and that is how the board will continue to refer clients to each other. Communication is also so important as a business owner. It is important to have your contacts stored in reliable CRM. Also, have those contacts stored in a reliable email campaign. You want your clients and board of directors to receive information about your products, services, news and how can they contact you if interested. Social media and consistency are key. If you can't automate the process using Hootsuite, delegate to a member of your team. If you think it doesn't add value to your business, eliminate. Do not waste your time as a business owner on items that do not deserve much time. You should balance revenue making activities versus non-revenue activities. For example, making phone calls, revenue making activity and entering prospective information in your CRM, not revenue-making activity. However, both are important. It is about finding the right balance for both of them. Have your board of directors and constantly keep them informed of your business for the latest news and trends.

Conclusion

I hope you enjoyed reading this book. It was a short how-to book for those who have challenges connecting with people and networking with individuals at networking events. I enjoyed writing this book to give the secrets of how I have successfully networked over the past decade for my previous employer and now for myself as an entrepreneur. My goal in writing this book is to help those who have challenges in networking and those who need to think outside of the box to network. The truth of the matter is everything everywhere is your network. Your baseball team, your church, your jiu-jitsu class, your child's parent at daycare are all examples of different networks that you may not realize you are a part of. I follow the law of reciprocity and try to help my network across the board. It is not just about referrals received, but also referrals are given. It's not just helping yourself but helping others.

I interviewed experts in networking, master networkers. I interviewed them so they can provide perspectives on how they leveraged networking in their everyday business and how it has made them successful in their roles with their companies or businesses today. By providing their perspectives, hopefully, it helps you come up with a strategy to improve and expand your network. FORMEA so important in networking (Family Occupation Recreation Motivation). I also added Education and Achievements to the acronym. Networking is about expanding your network and creating new ones to assist each other in your respective businesses.

I touched on techniques to organize your business cards, leveraging technology to store contact information and adding contacts to existing email campaigns. As a business owner, it is so important to have a system in place once you collect all of those business cards. Social Media presence and having strategic posts is so important as a business owner as well. I mentioned using Hootsuite for example as a social media management tool in sending a consistent message across all major social media platforms. I also touched on using LinkedIn to stay in touch with your network.

I hope this book helps in strategies to expand networking. Join a networking group, join a board, volunteer at a nonprofit. Using these strategies or tactics will assist in the expansion of your business. Your goal as an entrepreneur is to be exposed as much as possible where you'd like to be exposed.

Please let me know your progress. Email me at jairo@borjaconsultinggroup.com Do you think you still need some formal coaching? Reach out to me as well. I hope you enjoyed this book and apply these methods in your everyday business.

"Perfection is not attainable, but if we chase perfection, we can catch excellence." Vince Lombardi

Just me at the Statewide Hispanic Chamber of Commerce Business
Convention & Business Expo back in 2019.

With my friends from Corona Queens, NY, at my friend Manny's
wedding back in September of 2019.

With my friends Allan, Marc, Chris, Troy and George for Marc's
Birthday in October of 2019.

Rafael Mata Vice President of Business Development at GAMBIT
Services and I are supporting Luis De La Hoz Chairman Statewide
Hispanic Chamber of Commerce of New Jersey, who was honored
back on October 11th, 2019 by El Diario.

With Carlos Medina President and CEO Statewide Hispanic
Chamber of Commerce of New Jersey

Interviewing Luis De La Hoz Chairman for the Statewide Hispanic Chamber of Commerce of New Jersey for the book at Las Marias in New Brunswick, NJ. Photo Credit: Alejandro Roman

My daughter Emma at the Hogan Beach Shop in Orlando, FL for our Summer Vacation in 2019.

130

My lovely family at my graduation back in August of 2019.

From left to right, my brother Michael, mother Carmen, daughter
Emma, myself, and Stepfather, Lino at my graduation
in August of 2019.

With my mother Carmen and daughter Emma.

My lovely wife Sofia and amazing stepdaughter Emilie during my
graduation in August of 2019.

My daughter Emma and I on a ride at Busch Gardens for our
Summer Vacation 2019.

With my brother Michael at WrestleMania 35. Fun Fact, I've been to
16 WrestleManias.

Book Dr. Jairo Borja for Speaking Engagements

D r. Borja is available for speaking engagements at conferences or schools. For more information, please contact:

Dr. Jairo Borja
www.BorjaConsultingGroup.com
E-mail: jairo@borjaconsultinggroup.com

Follow Dr. Borja:
Facebook @drjairoborja
Twitter:@borjaconsulting
LinkedIn: @drjairoborjadba
Instagram @borjaconsultinggroup

TESTIMONIALS

"Motivation and positivity are at the forefront of Dr. Jairo Borja's book. A well-cultivated story with insight and tips for all. The text has a natural ability to enlighten young minds, captivate audiences. As an educator and professional, this book is going to enhance the lives of many.

Your net worth is your network, and this can only be cultivated one connection at a time."

Dr. Melissa Baralt
President of SheCaucus

"Dr. Jairo Borja is highly skilled at presenting, coaching, training, and inspiring people to action.

When he visited First Calvary Baptist Church in Brooklyn in 2018, he did a phenomenal job connecting with the group during his easy to understand and powerful Marketing Session."

Min. Marc Thompson
Director of Business Development, Berkeley College

"I've been working with Jairo for a few years now and must say he is so dedicated to assisting professionals in following their entrepreneurial journey. I thank him for guiding and supporting my business. This book is a great resource for those individuals pursuing to be entrepreneurs and wanting to learn the key success in networking."

Ashley Alba
President of Universal Executive Solutions

Made in the USA
Middletown, DE
12 November 2020